THE SETTLEMENT OF
LABOR DISPUTES ON
RIGHTS IN AUSTRALIA

THE SETTLEMENT OF LABOR DISPUTES ON RIGHTS IN AUSTRALIA

By Paul F. Brissenden

INSTITUTE OF INDUSTRIAL RELATIONS
UNIVERSITY OF CALIFORNIA · LOS ANGELES

Industrial Relations Monographs of the
Institute of Industrial Relations

Foreword

The Institute of Industrial Relations is pleased to offer *The Settlement of Labor Disputes on Rights in Australia* as the thirteenth volume in its Monograph Series. Paul F. Brissenden, the author of this work, is Professor Emeritus of Economics at Columbia University and has been Senior Visiting Scholar at the Institute of Advanced Projects, East-West Center, Honolulu. During a distinguished lifetime of research in industrial relations, Dr. Brissenden has published on a wide variety of issues. Among his earlier notable contributions are *The I.W.W.; A Study of American Syndicalism,* and *Earnings of Factory Workers 1899–1927, An Analysis of Pay-Roll Statistics.* More recently his time has been devoted to comparative studies of industrial relations practices in Australia, New Zealand, and the United States. Professor Brissenden's repeated visits to Australia and New Zealand may well lend special significance to his latest work presented herewith.

The Institute reading committee for this manuscript consisted of Irving Bernstein and Paul Prasow of UCLA, and myself. Anne P. Cook, Elaine Linden, and Felicitas Hinman were the editors. The cover was designed by Marvin Rubin.

The viewpoint expressed is that of the author and is not necessarily that of the Institute of Industrial Relations or of the University of California.

BENJAMIN AARON, *Director*
Institute of Industrial Relations
University of California, Los Angeles

Preface

In these pages are the results of an attempt to explain to American readers how the Australian systems of industrial arbitration are utilized to deal with industrial grievances, or labor disputes over rights. The major concern of the Australian arbitrators, disputes on interests, has been considered in *Settlement of Labor Disputes in Australia, New Zealand and the United States* (University of Hawaii, Industrial Relations Center, 1963). Since the Australian arbitral apparatus was built up as machinery for the settlement, primarily, of disputes over interests, and was utilized only later, and somewhat as an afterthought, for dealing with rights, it has seemed necessary to give some attention to the systems as a whole, and even to consider—perhaps too minutely—their utilization in disputes over interests. Not only is reliance in Australia in large measure upon the same apparatus for handling the two classes of disputes, but also the processes followed are often identical or closely similar.

Two Australian authorities—Professor Kingsley Laffer of the University of Sydney and Professor C. P. Mills of the same institution—have been kind enough to read the manuscript and give it the benefit of their knowledge of the Australian system which they know as I never can hope to know it. Errors and misapprehensions no doubt remain, but I feel sure that they are less numerous and less serious than they would have been without the acute and searching ministrations of these two experts. At many points the tenor of the text has been modified in accordance with their counsel. In other places, mostly in contexts in which my own (vulnerable) opinions have differed from theirs, I have ventured merely to set out their disagreeing comments in the margins. Except where otherwise indicated, the quoted comments from Professor Laffer are from his *Comments* dated August 18, 1965, and those from Professor Mills from his letter dated July 26, 1965. However handled, their suggestions have put me forever in debt to them, and I am grateful. Of course they are in no way responsible for the judgments made or the facts found herein.

Mr. Justice Sir Richard Kirby, President of the Commonwealth Conciliation and Arbitration Commission, Mr. Justice J. C. Moore, Deputy

President of the same tribunal, and Mr. Justice R. M. Eggleston, a judge of the Commonwealth Industrial Court, were good enough to examine and comment upon earlier drafts of the manuscript. I hope they will not conclude that they have commented in vain! In any case, what they have done is deeply appreciated.

During my visits to Australia, I was given such generous light and leading by so many other informed Australians that it seems inexpedient to name them. But without their patient tutoring this report would be even less adequate than it is.

The members of the staff of the Institute of Industrial Relations at the University of California, Los Angeles, have faced up—with skill and fortitude—to a manuscript which surely would drive ordinary editors crazy. I am deeply grateful to them, and to the members of the staff of the Industrial Relations Center at the University of Hawaii.

P. F. BRISSENDEN

Contents

Chapter 1
Introduction

This monograph deals with the settlement in Australia of industrial disputes over rights—often called grievance controversies. In general these disputes are local, minor, and *intraplant,* their characteristics being much the same in all industrialized countries. It must be emphasized that the class of disputes considered here makes up only a part— and much the less important part at that—of the whole body of industrial disputes dealt with by the Australian public tribunals. These "rights" disputes and the fashion of their handling are overshadowed by the arrangements made for the handling of major, contract, or "interest" disputes. Australians recognize that the rights controversies present problems; but, by and large, they have dealt with these matters through a system which they have built for coping with the controversies over interests. We will discuss the settlement of interest disputes only insofar as necessary to get some perspective on the moving parts in the Australian arbitral system and to see how they are brought to bear on rights disputes.

Our main inquiry into the Australian system is introduced by a summary description of the continent and the Commonwealth which occupies it. We then compare the arbitral process in Australia and the analogous process in the United States and note the peripheral nature of the role of collective bargaining in Australia. There follows a brief discussion of the origins and general features of the federal and state arbitral systems, and the "two-story" wage structure Down Under.[1]

The second chapter presents a description of the Australian arbitral apparatus in the federal jurisdiction and in the four state jurisdictions in which such machinery operates, with emphasis upon the state system in New South Wales. This description is followed by an examination of the important arrangements which have been made for coal mining, particularly in New South Wales, Queensland, and Western Australia. The next two chapters seek to explore the doctrines of interstateness and of ambit and the limitations these place upon the freedom of action

---

[1] The single word "arbitral," as used in these pages to describe the Australian system, is shorthand for "conciliative-arbitral."

of the tribunals in dealing with the wage structure, and upon a careful distinction between labor disputes on rights and those on interest.

Discussion of the operation of the arbitral apparatus occupies the largest section of the monograph. Here the analysis centers upon the principal channels and devices through which disputes on rights are dealt with, such as boards of reference, industrial magistrates, industrial courts, major tribunals, award making, award variation, collective bargaining, and industrial action. Seventeen cases, illustrating most of the methods and involving most of the classes of tribunals, are outlined in the hope that in this way some color of reality may be given to an exposition which otherwise might well seem somewhat fourth-dimensional. The final chapters, again, point up some differences and similarities between the Australian and the American systems and offer some concluding observations.

The Continent and the Commonwealth

Australia is about the size of the United States and, as will be noted, has now become no less highly industrialized. Yet its total population is just under eleven million. Industrial activities, as distinguished from agricultural and pastoral, are much less widely dispersed over its continental expanse than they are in this country. Manufacturing activities, in which about 30 percent of the workers are gainfully employed as compared with 22 percent in the United States,[2] are concentrated largely in a relatively narrow coastal belt in the southeast, running through the capital cities of four of the nation's six states: Adelaide (South Australia), Melbourne (Victoria), Sydney (New South Wales), and Brisbane (Queensland). These cities are all seaports and together account for six of the eleven million people. Sydney, with 2,216,000 people, is the largest industrial center, with Melbourne, 1,956,000 people, a close second. These two cities contain more than one-third of the population of Australia. While some eleven percent of the economically active population of the United States is employed by the federal or state governments, about twice that proportion of the Australian labor force is in government service, in which "... no less than one fifth of the [Australian]

---

[2] Official statistics published in this country show in the United States 16.2 million persons engaged in manufacturing out of a total of 71.3 million "economically active," and in Australia 1.1 million persons so engaged out of a total economically active population of 3.7 million. The figures, while not strictly comparable, i.e., U.S. data are for 1958, Australian for 1961, are believed to be adequate for the present purpose. They seem to warrant the conclusion that while 22 percent of the economically active American population are engaged in manufacturing, 30 percent are so engaged in Australia. *Statistical Abstract of the U.S.*, 1964. Commonwealth Bureau of Census and Statistics, *The Labour Report*, 1962–1963.

labor force is employed. . . ."[3] With such a small population, the domestic market is quite limited. Yet, as two Australian writers point out,

... the economy is highly industrialized in terms of employment, only 13 per cent of the work force being engaged in primary production, while 28 per cent are engaged in manufacturing. This compares with 12 and 27 per cent ... for the United States. . . . About 80 per cent of the work force are wage and salary earners. Of these about three-quarters are in private employment, the balance being employees of public authorities. . . . [A]ssociated with this industrialization is a very strong tendency toward urbanization, just over 80 per cent of the population living in cities. . . .[4]

In addition to the six states there are two (continental) federal territories: the Australian Capital Territory—Australia's "District of Columbia"—and the Northern Territory which occupies a large part of the continent's interior. Finally, to the north lie the Australian Territory of Papua and the Trust Territory of (east) New Guinea, both being parts of the island of New Guinea whose western end is a part of Indonesia.

Australia is the driest of the continents. All the Australian rivers combined have only half the flow of the Mississippi. Apart from its well-watered southeast rim, the continent is largely made up of the "out-back," or "back blocks." There are exceptions, notably the relatively small, heavily timbered area occupying the southwest corner of the continent. It is authoritatively reported that about forty percent of the country's area "receives less than ten inches of rain per annum and [that] the great bulk of the central area is unsuitable for settlement."[5]

In 1961 Australia, a member of the British Commonwealth of Nations, had a population of ten-and-a-half million, of whom 95 percent were "British."[6] Its government is similar to that of Britain; it has a bicameral parliament, established under the sanctions of a constitution shaped somewhat on the lines of that of the United States and giving rise to roughly analogous federal–state relations. The constitution, like that of the United States, assigns certain enumerated powers to the federal government. One of these is the commerce power, but in Australia this is not the source of the federal power to deal with labor disputes.

---

[3] Statistical Abstract of the U.S., 1964, pp. 216, 435; Colin McInnes and the Editors of Life, Australia and New Zealand (1964), p. 62.

[4] Peter H. Karmel and Maureen Brunt, The Structure of the Australian Economy (Melbourne: Cheshire, 1962), quoted by Gallagher, J., in Judgment, Basic Wage Inquiry (1964), at 35 (Print A 9600). Despite the relatively small proportion of the work force engaged in primary production, ". . . four fifths of all [Australian] exports are still agricultural . . ." Life World Library, Australia and New Zealand, p. 95.

[5] Karmel and Brunt, as cited by Gallagher, J., note 4 supra, Print A 9600, p. 35.

[6] The population classified as of June 30, 1961, as "British" was 9,983,634 in a grand total of 10,508,186. Commonwealth Year Book, 1963, p. 324. "In pursuance to established policy, the general practice is not to permit persons of non-European descent to enter Australia for the purpose of settling permanently. . . ." Ibid., p. 348.

ORIGIN AND NATURE OF THE AUSTRALIAN ARBITRAL SYSTEMS

The Commonwealth, or federal, authority to deal with labor disputes derives from the "industrial" power, conferred upon the Commonwealth Parliament by Section 51 (xxxv) of the constitution, which provides that the parliament "shall have power to make laws for the peace, order and good government of the Commonwealth with respect to . . . conciliation and arbitration for the prevention and settlement of industrial disputes extending beyond the limits of any one State."[7] It is under authority of this constitutional provision, which has never been amended, that the all-important federal arbitral tribunals have been created. This is the only constitutional reference to labor-dispute settlement. In 1904 the Australian Parliament duly enacted a law "with respect to . . . conciliation and arbitration," entitled the "Conciliation and Arbitration Act 1904." Although it has been amended many times, it stands today on the federal statute book in form and content closely similar to the original 1904 edition.

All systems, federal and state, rest upon a concept of the coverage of the term "industrial" which is much wider in scope than the same word used in the context of American industrial relations. The reach of the Australian tribunals extends much more widely into the professional and the lower and intermediate managerial sectors than in this country. Thus, bank officials in the lower and intermediate reaches and members of unions or associations are not infrequently parties to industrial disputes. A similar situation exists with respect to engineers, and perhaps also insurance officers, journalists, and theatre managers. Government employees, also, seem to be brought more within the reach of the Australian arbitral systems than they are in the United States. For example, Professor Edward I. Sykes of the University of Queensland points out that in one case the High Court of Australia "decided that an association could be registered [as a union and be a party to an industrial

[7] As an official publication of the parliament points out, ". . . there is no counterpart to par. (xxxv) in the United States or Canadian constitutions. Legislation under this paragraph has been therefore a unique experiment in the sphere of industrial relations." Parliament of the Commonwealth of Australia, *A Note on Some Aspects of Conciliation and Arbitration in the Commonwealth*, (Canberra: Commonwealth Government Printer, 1956), p. 4. The Australian Constitution is a statute (63 & 64 Vic. c. 12) enacted by the Parliament of Great Britain and Ireland on July 9, 1900. It became effective January 1, 1901. An official, indexed, text is available in pamphlet form, incorporating all alterations made through 1946: *Commonwealth of Australia, The Constitution and the Statute of Westminster Adaptation Act 1942* (Canberra: Government Printer, 1964). Its text also appears in Appendix C in Crisp, L.F., *The Parliamentary Government of the Commonwealth of Australia* (New Haven: Yale University Press, 1949).

dispute] even though it described the "industry of its members as 'The Local Government Municipal and Statutory Corporations Industry.' "[8]

The emergence of the Australian systems of compulsory arbitration in the first years of the twentieth century took place under circumstances which gave those systems from the outset an exclusive, or nearly exclusive, orientation to the adjustment of labor disputes on divergent interests rather than rights. In other words, the tribunals very early came to be concerned much more with the determination of working rules for the future than with alleviation of grievances arising out of those rules in operation. With the passage of time, with multiplication of awards and consequent multiplication of award-interpretation cases, major tribunals found themselves, perforce, dealing with such rights cases. Furthermore, before 1919 the problem of disputes "arising under" awards (i.e., rights disputes) had become sufficiently pressing to prompt the creation of boards of reference to deal with them.[9]

The evolution of the Australian systems is a complex story. When the Commonwealth of Australia was formed at the turn of the century, the new constitution in paragraph (xxxv) of Section 51, as noted above, bestowed upon the parliament the power to make laws with respect to "conciliation and arbitration for the prevention and settlement of industrial disputes extending beyond the limits of any one State." This is the principal source of Commonwealth industrial power. But national authority to deal with industrial relations also derives in a measure from the trade and commerce power. Paragraph (xxxv), Section 51, gives the national parliament power to deal with *industrial disputes,* and only by conciliation and arbitration, but not to deal with *industrial matters* in contexts where no disputes are involved. But the parliament may deal with industrial matters, even though no disputes are involved, and by means other than conciliation and arbitration, insofar as those matters relate to trade and commerce with other countries or have arisen "in a Territory of the Commonwealth."[10]

The parliament exercised this power by the enactment in 1904 of the Commonwealth Conciliation and Arbitration Act. That statute speaks of the prevention and settlement of industrial disputes as being among it "chief objects" (Section 2), but it does not define the reach and cover-

---

[8] "Labour Arbitration in Australia" (1964), 13 *American Journal of Comparative Law,* 216, at 238 (n. 47).

[9] According to Henry Bournes Higgins, for some seven years the president of the Court of Arbitration (now the Commission), "... the Act [§ 40a; now § 50(1)(a)] enables the Court to appoint 'Boards of Reference,' and such Boards involve opportunities for meeting for discussion of methods and alleged grievances...." A New Province for Law and Order," 32 *Harvard Law Review,* 189, 197 (January 1919).

[10] Conciliation and Arbitration Act, 1904–1964, § 82 (b).

age of the phrase "industrial disputes." Absent any explicit limitation upon the phrase, it seems arguable that it embraces disputes on rights as well as those on interest. The constitutional provision, however, does limit parliament in that it may not legislate with respect to intrastate disputes or nonindustrial disputes.

But what was the nature of the labor disputes envisaged in 1904 by the arbitral pioneers? What sort of differences was Justice Higgins, the second president of the Court of Arbitration, concerned about? It seems certain that the eminent jurist was thinking mostly—if not exclusively—about what are called in these pages labor disputes on interests, i.e., "fair and reasonable" rates of wages to pay the worker for his work tomorrow and the day after. "The 'basic' or living wage, the minimum wage for the unskilled worker," said Higgins, "is the primary factor in the fixing of all wages by award...."[11]

It does not appear that labor disputes about the meaning and application of award provisions—disputes "arising under"—were given more than cursory attention until years after the time of Higgins. The parties and the judges were completely absorbed by disputes over interests, and the arbitral machinery was set up deliberately to deal with such disputes. Later, questions naturally arose in multiplying numbers—in connection with transfer and dismissal cases and the like—about the meaning and application of the terms of the awards that had been made. These questions prompted the tribunals expediently to utilize the devices already at hand as means for dealing with these newly emerging disputes on rights.

However, with the multiplication of awards it must have become more and more apparent that special arrangements would have to be made to deal with disputes "arising under" awards. Boards of reference emerged to meet this need as early as 1915, and later ancillary agencies like the local coal authorities, which are partly referee tribunals, and the mine conciliation committees provided for in the twin Commonwealth–New South Wales coal statutes, were established.

In the five strictly arbitral jurisdictions—New South Wales, Queensland, South Australia, Western Australia, and the Commonwealth[12]—there are both common features and significant differences in the ways

---

[11] Higgins, op. cit., p. 199.

[12] The two wages board states of Victoria and Tasmania are here considered nonarbitral jurisdictions. Many Australian authorities, including Professor Kingsley Laffer, disagree with this judgment. He points out, moreover, that South Australia makes considerable use of wages boards, with two-thirds of its workers under their coverage. Certainly, one cannot classify South Australia as a "nonarbitral jurisdiction." Its system seems to be hybrid.

and means of arbitral settlement of industrial grievances and of labor disputes generally:

1) All five systems are sets of governmental arrangements for semicompulsory conciliation and compulsory arbitration. At the very least, the systems presume (and are built upon) the existence of organizations of employers and employees. It is perhaps more accurate to say that the systems require and encourage them.

2) In all of the major tribunals the arbitrators are public officials. Insofar as disputes are determined by one or another of the major tribunals, the parties do not, even indirectly, choose the persons who are to settle their disputes.[13]

3) In all five systems the existence of an industrial dispute is an important prerequisite to action by a tribunal. In the Commonwealth jurisdiction it is essential, and the dispute must be interstate. In the four state arbitral systems the existence of an "industrial matter" (which may or may not involve an industrial dispute) is a prerequisite.

4) In all five jurisdictions the primary concern (at least of the major tribunals) is a quasi-legislative preoccupation with labor disputes on interests. The major Australian tribunals, therefore, utilize devices shaped for use in the determination of what the working rules are to be in the future, deciding, in other words, what unions and employers in the United States decide by negotiation.

5) To put the matter negatively, the major Australian tribunals, insofar as they deal with minor, local, or grievance disputes, must do so, as best they can, under arrangements which do not appear to have been made with such disputes in mind.

6) Some of the ancillary tribunals, especially the boards of reference in the Commonwealth and Western Australian jurisdictions and the conciliation committees in New South Wales, have been conceived by the lawmakers, at least in some measure, as agencies for dealing with grievance disputes—the most important category of "disputes over rights." That expression, however, is not used Down Under; the phrase "disputes arising under this award," commonly used in Australian awards, also includes disputes over interests.

7) Common to all five arbitral jurisdictions is the phenomenon of a two-story structure of award wages: There is the foundational minimum "basic wage," which is the same in all industries but varies geographically. Superimposed upon the basic-wage foundation is a second-story system of minimum marginal wages which vary with the degree of skill, if any, required, and which, therefore, tend to vary as between one industry or job classification and another.

8) Finally, to the two-story award structure must be added a third story represented by over-award payments made unilaterally by employers or bargained out between union and employers, and received by most employees other than those working for government agencies.

---

[13] Until 1963 the major arbitral tribunal of Western Australia, the Industrial Court, was of the tripartite sort in which *ex parte* members were designated by union and employer groups respectively. Some of the ancillary tribunals are tripartite; among these are most of the boards of reference of the Western Australian and Commonwealth jurisdictions, and the conciliation committees in New South Wales.

Not surprisingly, the Australian systems of industrial arbitration have been the subject of extensive criticisms by Australians. For example, one well-informed writer has remarked that "not even body-line bowling has caused as much discussion as compulsory arbitration."[14] As is to be expected, not all of this criticism is laudatory. The same writer suggests that ". . . there are economic objections in plenty to the system. Not for twenty years [he states] were real wages permanently increased. In 1927 they were only 7.5 percent higher than in 1911." And he suggests that ". . . the greatest disability of the whole system is the existence of the Commonwealth Arbitration Court [now the Conciliation and Arbitration Commission] side-by-side with the wage-fixing tribunals of the different states."[15] "The existing jumble of competing authorities has resulted in a huge game of hide and seek, in which perspiring union secretaries run after judges suspected of radicalism, while equally perspiring company lawyers endeavor to head them off."[16]

THE WAGE STRUCTURE: BASIC WAGE AND MARGINS

The basic wage, as defined in the federal legislation, is "that wage, or that part of a wage, which is just and reasonable for an adult male, without regard to any circumstances pertaining to the work upon which, or the industry in which, he is employed."[17] This underlying wage, referred to by Justice Higgins as "the 'basic' or living wage," was until 1953 automatically adjusted "in accordance with variations . . . in retail price index numbers," and issued quarterly.[18] It is now determined not directly on the basis of living costs (the *needs* basis), but in accordance with the economic capacity of the economy as a whole, the automatic quarterly adjustment having been discontinued. Basic wage rates, generally resting on and not lower than the federal determinations, are regularly fixed in all of the states.[19] In the Basic Wage Inquiries held

---

[14] Portus, G. V., *Australia: An Economic Interpretation* (2nd ed., Sydney: 1933), p. 80.
[15] *Ibid.*
[16] *Id.* p. 82. All this is not unlike the "game of hide and seek" which ensues when American employers approach the judges for injunctions in labor disputes involving their employees. See Brissenden, "Campaign Against the Labor Injunction," *American Economic Review*, March, 1933.
[17] Conciliation and Arbitration Act, 1904–1964, § 33(1)(b). There is a parallel definition in § 33(1)(d) of the basic wage for adult females, now fixed at 75 percent of the basic rate for males.
[18] Commonwealth Bureau of Census and Statistics, *The Labour Report*, 1959, p. 36.
[19] Federal award rates do not automatically apply intrastate, but actually there is a close correspondence, the state tribunals tending generally to adjust their rates to federal levels. Moreover, there is pressure upon the state tribunals so to conform. The federal Conciliation and Arbitration Act, 1904–1964, provides in Section 65 that where a state award is inconsistent with a federal determination, the former is invalid and the latter prevails. State award rates above comparable federal rates are not deemed

from time to time, separate determinations are made for adult males and adult females. Separate federal basic rates are fixed for each of the six capitals, Sydney, Melbourne, Brisbane, Adelaide, Perth, and Hobart and, overall, for the six capitals combined. Originally a needs basic wage, it is now generally accepted "that the wage should be fixed at the highest amount which the economy can sustain and that the 'dominant factor' is the capacity of the community to carry the resultant wage levels."[20] (It appears that automatic quarterly adjustments now continue only in New South Wales.)

The "award wage" is the basic wage plus any marginal wage for the particular occupation. The latter, in the federal jurisdiction, is fixed only by a commissioner. The basic wage in that jurisdiction may be altered or fixed in the first instance only by the Conciliation and Arbitration Commission in "presidential session," that is, sitting *en banc* with three or more judges. In New South Wales the federal judgments are legislatively incorporated.[21] The other three arbitral states (Queensland, South Australia, and Western Australia) declare basic wage rates from time to time. These rates in any case are usually the same, or nearly the same, as the federal rates. South Australia adheres, by legislative enactment, to the Commonwealth basic wage. In Victoria the wages boards are required by statute to take into consideration the relevant awards of the federal Commission in fixing the basic wage. The Tasmanian wages boards in 1961 incorporated in their determinations the basic wage rates awarded by the federal Commission in that year.[22]

The president of the Commonwealth Conciliation and Arbitration Commission, Sir Richard Kirby, has pointed out that the "decisions of the Commission in regard to the basic wage, standard hours of work . . . long-service leave and the like," made as they are after regularly held full-bench hearings, in effect "are part of one constant continuing case rather than the series of separate cases they appear in outward form. . . ."[23] His Honour speaks of them as "national cases," as distin-

inconsistent. It seems that state award rates are rarely, if ever, lower than the federal rates. (See the statistics of basic wage rates under Commonwealth and state awards, *Industrial Information Bulletin*, January, 1964, pp. 63–69. The January issues of this *Bulletin* appear to carry these figures regularly.)
[20] Quoted in *Labour Report*, 1961, p. 82 (from 77 *Commonwealth Arbitration Reports* (hereafter cited as *CAR*) 494). The rates are published in the January issues of the *Industrial Information Bulletin*, which lists also the basic wage rates declared "under state awards." See generally on "Basic Wages in Australia," *Labour Report*, 1961, pp. 82–130. Similar data appear in *Labour Report*, 1961, pp. 235–244.
[21] Industrial Arbitration Act, 1940–1959, Part V, especially Section 55(1).
[22] *Labour Report*, 1961, pp. 118–130.
[23] "Some Comparisons between Compulsory Arbitration and Collective Bargaining," *The Journal of Industrial Relations* (Sydney), March, 1965, p. 1.

guished from what might loosely be called "local cases" which come before individual commissioners.[24]

"Wage margins" have been defined officially as "Minimum amounts awarded above the basic wage to particular classifications of employees for the features attaching to their work which justify payments above the basic wage, whether those features are the skill or experience required for the performance of that work, its particularly laborious nature, or the liabilities attached to its performance."[25] Margins traditionally have been keyed to the marginal rate determined for the classification of "fitter" in the *Metal Trades Award,* which, in turn, is fixed in terms of the value of the work done by him. The work values and the corresponding marginal rates for other classifications, in that award and in other federal awards as well, are fixed in relation to the fitter's rate prevailing at any given time. All this involves the very formidable business of fixing a valuation for the work of the metal trades fitter, and the no less formidable enterprise of determining the "relativities" of the work values of the myriad other skilled jobs to the work value of the fitter's job.[26]

Margins may be altered in the Commonwealth jurisdiction by a single member of the Commission, or indirectly, on appeal by a full bench constituted of at least three members, at least one of whom must be a judge. As has been noted, in all Australian jurisdictions the total minimum award wage rate is the sum of the basic rate and the marginal rate, which may be further increased by over-award payments negotiated or unilaterally granted by employers.

---

[24] *Ibid.,* p. 28. This writer recognizes that his characterization of the "nonarbitral" matters handled by indivdiual commissioners as "local cases" is objectionable. It is to be noted that His Honor does not use the expression. Some of them, such as most of the grievance cases, are undoubtedly local, or intrastate, and perhaps for this reason untouchable by a federal arbitrator. Many of the cases, like those in which the commissioner must make a new award or vary an old one, have wide-ranging "national" effects. Indeed, the constitutional necessity for "interstateness" would seem to bar the commissioner from handling cases that are "local" in the sense of being intrastate, although now and then federal arbitrators as noted elsewhere have been burned by such handling.

[25] Judgment [Commonwealth Arbitration Commission], *Metal Trades (re Margins),* 80 *CAR* 24.

[26] See J. R. Kerr, "Work Value," 6 *The Journal of Industrial Relations* (Sydney) 1, March 1964.

Chapter 2

The Apparatus and Its Functioning

The Australian arrangements are marshaled, not in a single system, but in a congeries of systems.[1] The most important ones stem from laws labeled "Conciliation and Arbitration" or "Industrial Arbitration," enacted by the parliaments of the five "arbitral" jurisdictions: the Commonwealth and the four states of New South Wales, Queensland, South Australia, and Western Australia. These arrangements have resulted in a dual federal–state apparatus, with the four state systems operative within their respective boundaries and the Commonwealth system responsible for the determination of interstate disputes in all six states and in the federal territories. The five sets of statutes confer upon courtlike tribunals—called either courts or commissions—the power to arbitrate industrial, that is, labor-management, disputes not settled through negotiation or direct action by the parties or by conciliation, and to make awards giving effect to their determinations. The arrangements are fundamentally similar in all five arbitral jurisdictions, all of them being compulsory governmental systems of tribunals manned by public officials in whose selection the parties to disputes have no direct voice.

The tribunals are largely staffed by judges. With two possible exceptions (in Western Australia and in Queensland[2]) the president of the

---

[1] The writer has been assisted in his effort to outline the Australian systems by the informative description of them by Mr. D. C. Thomson, Senior Lecturer in Law at the University of Sydney: "A Survey of Australian Industrial Tribunals," *Industrial Law Review*, July, 1955. On wages boards see E. R. Gwyther, Director, Industrial Relations Division, Victorian Employers' Federation: "Wages Boards: the System of Industrial Regulation in Victoria and Tasmania," *Business Review*, February, 1962. ("Paper presented to the Industrial Officers' Conference, Sydney, September 1961. . . .")

[2] In Queensland there are two tribunals: a five-man award-making Industrial Conciliation and Arbitration Commission, none of whose members is required to be a judge, and an Industrial Appeal Court, whose president (and only member) must be a judge of the State Supreme Court. Late in 1963 the arbitral system of Western Australia was completely overhauled. The tripartite (three-man) Court of Arbitration was replaced by a four-man Industrial Commission whose (lay) members are appointed by the governor, and an Industrial Appeal Court, constituted of three judges.

Professor Laffer points out that the members of the Queensland and Western Australian Commissions are not judges, that the Commonwealth Commission has a number of non-presidential members who are laymen, and that "the trend appears to be away from judges" in respect to "non-judicial functions."

award-making, as distinguished from the adjudicatory, tribunal is required to be a judge, and all members of the Commonwealth Industrial Court are judges. The Industrial Commission of New South Wales is constituted entirely of judges. Whether judges or not, all members of the principal tribunals are governmentally appointed. In all jurisdictions stress is placed upon conciliation and upon the importance of exhausting conciliative efforts before the dispute "goes into court" or is "referred to arbitration." Both conciliation and arbitration are compulsory, conciliation being so in the sense of compulsion to confer, and arbitration in the sense of compulsion both to appear and give evidence before the tribunal and to give effect to whatever award may be prescribed. As already noted, the grist of the tribunals is made up predominantly not of rights disputes over the meaning or application of the working rules, but of interests controversies over what the rules are to be. The federal commissioners deal in one way or another with a good many rights disputes.

The most important exception to this nearly exclusive orientation of the tribunals to the determination of disputes on interests was the early appearance in the Commonwealth and in one or two state jurisdictions of ancillary tribunals called boards of reference. In coal mining there also emerged minor tribunals, the mine conciliation committees and local coal authorities. Although the functioning of these ancillary agencies has not been explicitly defined in the enabling statutes as the settlement of rights disputes, their activities have been predominantly concerned with such disputes. The boards are bound by instruction in their respective awards to settle "disputes arising out of" those awards.[3] The committees, similarly, are under a duty spelled out in the twin statutes "to deal with all industrial grievances arising at the coal mine."[4]

The Australian arbitral apparatus functions, it seems, in a context in which there is a certain—sometimes a large—amount of collective bargaining. The collective negotiations may take place before, during, and after resort to the tribunals. In some industries they may be quite extensive and protracted, whether in the preliminary or the postliminary phase. Prearbitral negotiations seemingly are not unlike those incident to labor-contract making in America. Postarbitral bargaining is likely to center on the determination of over-award wage payments. This writer is disposed to think of collective bargaining as a fringe process in Australia, but Professor Laffer does not share this view. He

---

[3] For example, Coal Mining Industry (Miners) Award, Queensland, 1954. (*CR* [Coal Reports?] (hereafter cited as *CR*) 1057) Clause 21.

[4] Commonwealth Coal Industry Act, 1946–1956, § 43(a); New South Wales Coal Industry Act, 1946–1951, § 49(a).

doubts "whether it is any longer reasonable" to regard it in this light, and suggests that compulsory arbitration "provides the base and collective bargaining (perhaps not strictly *collective* bargaining) the extremely important superstructure ... of over-award payments." It cannot be doubted that collective bargaining is important in Australia. But its importance there is marginal rather than central. This is to be expected since there is no legal compulsion upon Australian employers to bargain as there is upon American employers who, at least in the federal jurisdiction, can refuse only at their peril to bargain collectively with any union representing a majority of their employees in an "appropriate unit."[5] It seems to be only rarely in Australia that collective bargaining takes place before even the filing of claims, i.e., wholly outside of the system. Once within the system by virtue of claims filed, what bargaining goes on proceeds in the "conciliative prenumbra" of the system, stopping short at the point where the dispute is "referred into arbitration." Beyond that point there is little or no bargaining. Moreover, the bargaining that takes place in the "conciliative prenumbra" is more than bilateral; it is triangular, with the commissioner in the third corner. It is assisted, or supervised, bargaining.

The arbitral system in Australia, Professor Laffer suggests, "was developed to provide machinery for settling disputes regardless of whether they were interests or rights disputes." He goes on to say: "I think this is important for the understanding of our system, even though the way ... [it] developed with its emphasis on uniformity in wages and conditions gave ... [it] ... an interests orientation. The continued heavy reliance on informal processes [outside of the arbitral system] for dealing with grievances has also played its part in this ... orientation, which arises from the characteristics of the system rather than from weaknesses in the machinery—with determination of grievances as merely an afterthought."

THE FEDERAL SYSTEM

The principal federal tribunals, set up under four different statutes, are:

Commonwealth Conciliation and Arbitration Commission
Commonwealth Industrial Court
Public Service Arbitrator
Coal Industry Tribunal
Stevedoring Industry Authority

---

[5] Section 8(a)(5), Labor-Management Relations (Taft-Hartley) Act, 61 Stat. 156 (1947), 29 USC, § 185 (1958).

Ancillary to the Commission, and provided for in the Conciliation and Arbitration Act which created it, are:

>Boards of Reference, and
>Local Industrial Boards[6]

Similarly provided for in the law creating the Coal Industry Tribunal (Coal Industry Act, 1946–1956) are:

>Mine Conciliation Committees, and
>Local Coal Authorities

The Commonwealth Conciliation and Arbitration Commission is the chief federal award-making agency. The late Mr. Justice Alfred W. Foster, a deputy president of the Commission for many years, observed that "this tribunal . . . is by deliberate legislative policy, not a court," and noted also that "The decisions [by the Commission] to vary the basic wage is legislation for the future," enacted by "a quasi-legislative body."[7] The Commission presently is made up of seventeen commissioners of whom six are judges called "presidential members" (the president and five deputy presidents). The other eleven members are lay commissioners.[8] The work of the Commission is done by an extraordinarily variegated series of "benches" or "panels." Also, applications for awards may be heard and determined by any commissioner, sitting

[6] "Local Industrial Board" means "a Conciliator," "a State Industrial Authority willing to act," or a Local Board constituted as . . . directed by the Commission and consisting of equal numbers of representatives of employers and employees. Section 44(3).

[7] In Judgment, *Basic Wage Inquiry*, 1959, 91 *CAR* 706 (Print A 6618, pp. 26, 29, 32). Although the making and varying of awards is "legislation for the future" the court (now the Commission) which makes them has observed that it is "neither a social nor an economic legislature" and that although the exercise of its powers had widespread social and economic results it was "not the function of the Court to aim at such social and economic changes as may seem desirable to [its] members. . . ." (1952–1953 *Basic Wage and Standard Hours Inquiry* 77 *CAR* at 506). Years later the Commission said: "We are not national economic policy makers or planners" (97 *CAR* at 380). But in the High Court, Dixon, C.J., suggested that ". . . it would be absurd to suppose that . . . [the Commission] was to proceed blindly in its work of industrial arbitration and ignore the industrial, social and economic consequences of what it was invited to do. . . ." *The Queen v. Kelly*, 89 *Commonwealth Law Reports* (hereafter cited as *CLR*) 461, at 474. An award of the Commission, the High Court had said much earlier, was "in the nature of a legislative act" (per Isaacs and Rich, J.J., in *Waterside Workers Federation v. Gilchrist, Watt and Sanderson, Ltd.*, 34 *CLR* at 528). And the Commission itself noted that ". . . an award of this . . . [tribunal] is therefore an ordinance rather than a judgment; . . . the Court acts as a quasi-legislator and not as a Court in the strict sense. . . ." (the Full Court in the *Railways* case, 30 *CAR* at 767).

[8] *Eighth Annual Report of the President of the Commonwealth Conciliation and Arbitration Commission* (for year ended August 13, 1964) at 3. *The Labour Report*, 1961, states (p. 45) that the "Commission is . . . composed of a President, five Deputy Presidents, a Senior Commissioner, eight Commissioners and three Conciliators." This may be an error as to the conciliators; the *Eighth Annual Report* does not include conciliators as members of the tribunal. The president of the Commission speaks of "the Conciliators who are appointed pursuant to the Act but are not members of the Commission." *Eighth Annual Report* at 11.

alone as "the Commission" or by one or another of the panels. But special situations call for special "benches":

1) Applications pertaining to the basic-wage standard hours, or long-service leave, must be heard by the "Commission in Presidential Session," i.e., by a panel made up of at least three presidential members nominated by the president. A fair construction of the Act seems to warrant the conclusion that all other claims (of which the most important are applications for changes in marginal wage rates) are normally heard by single commissioners, with due allowance for appeal.

2) Should a commissioner be confronted with a case which he thinks should be handled by a panel, the president may, after consulting with the commissioner, arrange for its handling by a panel of not less than three members nominated by the president (at least one of them to be a presidential member, and one "where practicable, the commissioner concerned").

3) Appeals against awards made by single commissioners must be heard by "the Commission constituted by not less than three members . . . nominated by the President, of whom at least two are presidential members. . . ."[9]

The Commission is charged with responsibility for the settlement of industrial disputes.[10] This responsibility attaches, of course, with respect to all interstate industrial disputes, whether they are single, run-of-the-mill, and more or less simple, disagreements (over either rights or interests) with no direct impact beyond the industries immediately involved, or whether they are Basic-Wage-Inquiry matters with their wide-ranging repercussions throughout the Commonwealth. Yet it must be noted quickly that the Commission's functions, again as a by-product of institutional evolution, have now come to involve something significantly more than litigious dispute-settling, important as that function continues to be. This is particularly true of its Basic Wage Inquiries. The Commission may act "of its own motion," "is not bound by any rules of evidence," and may inform its mind as it thinks fit.[11] These powers, to be sure, apply to all of its proceedings, but they appear to have come to be exercised more fully and more potently in the Basic-Wage-Inquiry proceedings than in the more ordinary run-of-the-mill cases.

An important and significant aspect of the work of the federal Commission is that of three officials who are not members of that tribunal: the conciliators appointed by the governor-general under authority

---

[9] Conciliation and Arbitration Act, 1904–1964, §§ 33–35.

[10] "If no agreement . . . as to an industrial dispute is arrived at, the Commission shall . . . determine [that is to say, arbitrate] the dispute." *Ibid.*, § 32.

[11] Conciliation and Arbitration Act, 1904–1964, §§ 24; 40(1)(b). Although the Commission may act of its own motion, it may not so act except in the context of confrontation with an "industrial dispute, actual, impending or probable." It therefore may not make an inquiry except in such a dispute context.

of Section 19 of the Conciliation and Arbitration Act. The president of the Commission, Sir Richard Kirby, in his most recent *Annual Report,* has stressed the importance which the Commission attaches to the conciliative process.[12] After referring to the emphasis placed on conciliation by the Commission and its members, Sir Richard points out that "the Conciliators are appointed with the direct aim of putting [further] emphasis on conciliation."[13]

The conciliators are authorized to give assistance to the parties to enable them to reach amicable agreements. To effectuate this purpose a commissioner "may, if, in his opinion, it may assist the parties to an industrial dispute to settle . . . [it] by amicable agreement, and shall, if the parties . . . so request, arrange . . . for a Conciliator to be made available. . . . Where a Conciliator . . . [thus made available] is satisfied that the parties are unlikely to reach an amicable agreement, he shall . . . furnish a report . . . to the Commissioner as to the result of the endeavour to reach agreement. . . . A Conciliator shall not furnish [such] a report unless the parties . . . consent and agree upon its terms."[14] The statute continues: "A Conciliator made available . . . [as above] may, where the parties . . . [1] are unable to reach agreement on a part of the . . . dispute, [2] request him to determine that part . . . and [3] agree to abide by his decision, decide that part of the . . . dispute."[15] These arrangements evidently provide, first, for voluntary settlement, failing which there is (by Section 30(4)) compulsory arbitration. For good measure Section 32 of the Act provides: "If no agreement between the parties as to an industrial dispute is arrived at, the Commission shall . . . determine the dispute."

In all contexts, whether it be a Basic-Wage-Inquiry proceeding or the dismissal of a single employee, the Commission's business is to consider and resolve claims brought before it in labor-dispute cases. It is the dominant arbitral forum in the federal jurisdiction. Indeed, it seems fair to say that this (award-making) tribunal is the most important arbitral agency in Australia.

As noted above, there are other important forums in the Commonwealth jurisdiction: the (award-interpreting) Commonwealth Industrial Court, the Public Service Arbitrator, the Stevedoring [waterside] Industry Authority, and the Coal Industry Tribunal; the latter agency functions also (under identical Commonwealth and New South Wales statutes) in respect to intrastate disputes in the state of New South

---

[12] *Eighth Annual Report, op. cit.,* at 11.
[13] *Ibid.*
[14] Conciliation and Arbitration Act, 1904–1964, § 30(1)(2)(3).
[15] *Ibid.,* § 30(4).

Wales. These four agencies are all, primarily, award-making tribunals. Finally, it should be emphasized that no industrial dispute is appropriate matter for any Commonwealth tribunal unless it is interstate.

THE STATE SYSTEMS

The "strictly arbitral" state systems operate in four of the six states: New South Wales, South Australia, Queensland and Western Australia. Some Australian authorities even classify the "wages board" states of Victoria and Tasmania as arbitral jurisdictions.[16] At any rate the Australian apparatus, overall, includes both the comprehensive Commonwealth system and the state systems. The more important units in these systems are identified below.

Using the word "arbitration" in the widest sense, it fairly may be said that each of the six Australian states has an arbitral system for dealing with intrastate industrial disputes. However, Victoria and Tasmania use the wages-board technique, which is significantly different from the arbitral-court techniques used by the other four states and which some authorities do not consider really arbitral. The two wages board states, therefore, are considered separately. (South Australia's pattern is mixed; that state sometimes is referred to as a third wages board state.) In the four "arbitral" states the tribunals, their powers and their functioning, run substantially parallel to the "arbitral way" in the Commonwealth.

The most important state group is that of New South Wales, whose dominant arbitral agency is the Industrial Commission. Important also are the numerous tripartite, award-making conciliation committees, set up industry by industry, like the wages boards of Victoria and Tasmania. In New South Wales there is also a Crown Employees' Appeal Board and the Commonwealth–New South Wales Coal Industry Tribunal already mentioned. That tribunal is set up jointly under two statutes: the federal Coal Industry Act, 1946–1956 and the New South Wales Coal Industry Act, 1946–1951. The twin enactments both provide for local coal authorities with functions somewhat like those of boards of reference. Each authority consists "of a person appointed to be a Local Coal Authority, as chairman . . . and of two or three other . . . [representative] members. . . ."[17] The twin laws also provide for bipartite mine conciliation committees having power "to deal with all industrial grievances arising at the coal mine."[18] The local coal authorities have power

[16] See n. 23, *infra*.
[17] Federal Act, § 37(A)(1); New South Wales Act, § 43(A)(1).
[18] Federal Act, §§ 42, 43(a); New South Wales Act, §§ 48, 49(a).

to "settle any local industrial dispute or matter," including grievance disputes referred to them by the mine conciliation committees.[19] Clearly there are here two separate sets of tribunals, both of which appear to have power to deal with local disputes. The kinds of controversies, however, whether "local industrial disputes" or "industrial grievances arising at the coal mine," seem less clearly distinguishable.

In Queensland the Industrial Conciliation and Arbitration Commission and the Industrial Appeal Court function, respectively, in the same way as the similarly named Commonwealth agencies.

In South Australia there are: an Industrial Court which both makes and interprets awards, a Board of Industry, a large number of industrial boards,[20] and an award-making Public Service Arbitrator.

In Western Australia there is a system of tribunals more elaborate than in any other jurisdiction. The more important are the award-making Western Australian Industrial Commission constituted of four "non-representative" lay commissioners, and an Industrial Appeal Court of three judges. There are also the tripartite, award-making Government School Teachers' Tribunal, the Railways Classification Board, and the Western Australian Coal Industry Tribunal. Finally there are tripartite boards of reference, both for intrastate industry at large and for coal mining. Not only the tribunals, but evidently also the tripartite boards of reference (at least in mining) may make awards in settlement of disputes.[21]

The two wages board states—Victoria and Tasmania—are so called because their all-important industrial tribunals are their hundreds of tripartite "wages boards," set up industry by industry and numbering, in 1955, upwards of two hundred in Victoria and seventy-six in Tasmania. In these two states labor disputes are settled, not by juridical "law-making" as in the four arbitral jurisdictions, but by a process of dispute determination more like the multipartite parliamentary process characteristic of legislatures. The wages boards legislate on the basis of compromise among party groups. It is perhaps a significant difference between wages-board settlement of controverted matters and such settlement in ordinary parliaments that in the latter the settlement of all

---

[19] Federal Act, § 38(1); New South Wales Act, § 44(1).

[20] Apparently the industrial boards are assigned only limited powers (or powers over only limited groups of workers) in respect to parts of the state outside the metropolitan area. These boards are analogous to the wages boards of Victoria and Tasmania.

[21] Mining Act, 1904–1957, §§ 318, 231(1)(b) and 325. It is not clear to this writer whether all of the Western Australian boards of reference, or only those in coal mining, have award-making power.

kinds of disputes is by compromise hammered out among several party groups, while in the case of the wages boards industrial disputes *only* are adjusted by negotiation and settlement between the *two* groups making up the representative membership of the boards: viz. representatives respectively of employers and of unions of their employees.

Opinions differ as to the role of the wages boards, but there is good reason for regarding them as arbitral tribunals. For some differing opinions on this score, see the early case of the *Australian Boot Trade Employees Federation and Whybrow and Company,*[22] and a later proceeding (before the Commonwealth Court of Conciliation and Arbitration) involving the Graziers Association of Victoria and two Victorian wages boards. In the *Graziers* case the court (now the Commission) said: "We have come to the view, on an examination of the State Act under which these two [Wages] Boards have been appointed, that they have authority to exercise powers of arbitration with reference to industrial disputes."[23] In accord with this view is Professor Orwell de R. Foenander of the University of Melbourne, a leading Australian observer of the operations of the Australian arbitral systems. He indicated to this writer that in his judgment the wages boards were clearly authorized to resort to arbitration. He said, however, that he did not think that those tribunals, as a matter of practice, had acted under that authorization.[24] In one of his books Professor Foenander has elaborated further on the functions of the Australian wages boards:

In Australia [he says], the expression 'industrial arbitration' is employed to include the activities of Victorian and Tasmanian wages boards, although the method of those bodies is fully legislative as distinct from arbitral. A wages board does not perform the function of an arbitrator in a dispute that has arisen in industry. On the other hand, an industrial court acts—at least formally—as an arbitrator where employers . . . and organized labour are involved in labour disputes. Unlike that of a wages board, the jurisdiction of an industrial court is founded on a dispute. It will be seen, therefore, that the trade union—and to a lesser degree the employer organization—is an integral in labour arbitration, whereas it is not essential in the scheme of wages boards.[25]

The two "non-arbitral" states have tribunals in addition to their all-important wages boards. Victoria has a tripartite Industrial Appeals Court to deal with appeals from the determinations of the wages boards,

[22] 10 *Commonwealth Law Reports* 266, at 289.
[23] *The Graziers Assn. of Victoria v. The Shearing Industry [Wages] Board and the Agricultural and Pastoral Workers' Board* (Print No. A 4660), 82 *CAR* 57, at 59–60 (Dispute No. 450 of 1955).
[24] Personal interview, Melbourne, October 7, 1960.
[25] Orwell de R. Foenander, *Industrial Regulation in Australia* (Melbourne: University Press, 1947), p. 175.

a tripartite Teachers' Tribunal, and boards of reference.[26] Tasmania has an award-making Public Service Tribunal.[27] Finally, it must be emphasized that one of the four "arbitral" states, South Australia, also makes wide use of wages boards.

THE TRIBUNALS AND THE KINDS OF DISPUTES

These are the tribunals in the seven jurisdictions. But it must be noted that they were created under conditions which foredoomed them to serve in the prevention and settlement of industrial disputes without distinction (except as to interstateness) as to the nature of the dispute. As the systems developed, the tribunals found themselves dealing not so much (if at all) with the minor, intraplant controversies on rights as with the larger, more obtrusive, disputes which turned mostly on clashing interests and whose very nature required legislative treatment even if it was to be by judges. The disputes over rights, mostly small and local, tended to pass relatively unnoticed. Hence the systems evolved as arrays of tribunals mostly concerning themselves, in a process of "legislative" adjudication, with major disputes on interests rather than dealing judicially with minor disputes on rights. Most of the Australian tribunals continue to function in substantially this fashion. However, in recent years, some of them have been legislatively remodelled in a fashion more neatly to adapt the apparatus to the type of dispute.

Thus the parliaments of the Commonwealth, Queensland, and Western Australia have modified the tribunal arrangements in their several jurisdictions to specialize them in significant measure for dealing with industrial disputes of different kinds. The Commonwealth Parliament, in 1956, created a Commonwealth Industrial Court to make interpretations of awards and to enjoin breaches of the Act or of awards, and so forth.[28] At the same time the parliament restricted the Conciliation and Arbitration Commission more narrowly to the business of award-

---

[26] The Teachers' Tribunal consists of a chairman and a member representing the government of Victoria (both appointed by the governor), and a member elected by the teachers. (Teaching Service Act 1958, § 5.) The boards of reference in Victoria (Labour and Industry Act, 1958, cls. 3 and 31) are "constituted pursuant to a determination of a Wages Board. . . ." They are tripartite, with the chairman of the wages boards serving as chairman of the boards of reference.

[27] Public Service Tribunal Act 1958 (No. 78 of 1958). The foregoing enumeration is not exhaustive by any means. Thus Professor E. I. Sykes speaks of "satellite magisterial tribunals, composed of industrial magistrates, in New South Wales, Queensland and Western Australia." Edward I. Sykes, *Strike Law in Australia* (Sydney: Law Book Co. of Australasia, 1960), p. 20. There is also an Australian Capital Territory Industrial Board, a federal agency, in Canberra.

[28] Conciliation and Arbitration Act, 1904–1964, §§ 109, 110, 117, 150. It is not clear to this writer to what extent the Stevedoring Industry Authority, the Public Service Arbitrator or the Coal Industry Tribunal deal with minor disputes (on rights). There seems to be no doubt that their prime concern is with disputes on interests, but all of

making. Somewhat similar legislative amendments in Queensland and Western Australia have resulted in shifts in the tribunal arrangements calculated to bring about the same sort of specialization. In terms of the dichotomy of emphasis favored in these pages, it would seem appropriate to say that the effect of these legislative changes has been to adapt the arbitral machinery in the three jurisdictions named to the separate handling of disptues on rights and interests, respectively. Specifically, the Commonwealth Conciliation and Arbitration Commission has become a tribunal more exclusively concerned with settlement of industrial disputes on interests, while the Commonwealth Industrial Court is primarily concerned with disputes on rights. Similar separations of function mark the Queensland Industrial Conciliation and Arbitration Commission in relation to that state's Industrial Court, and (perhaps) the Western Australian Industrial Commission in relation to its Industrial Appeal Court.

The tribunals in the other two arbitral states, New South Wales and South Australia, are less specialized in respect to the type of disputes dealt with. The Industrial Commission of New South Wales takes on industrial disputes of whatever kind, and the same seems true of that state's conciliation committees which appear to function somewhat like wages boards.[29] The Industrial Court of South Australia, also, evidently both makes and interprets awards, thus dealing with disputes involving both interests and rights. That state's industrial boards, built and functioning like the wages boards of Victoria and Tasmania, also appear to deal with disputes on interests and on rights.[30]

In the wages board states of Victoria and Tasmania, it appears that the boards handle all kinds of industrial disputes, although it may be that grievance disputes get relatively little attention. To the extent, of course, that the wages boards fail—if they do fail—to deal with rights disputes, such controversies would seem to be unprovided for in

---

them (except perhaps the Public Service Arbitrator) appear to handle some rights disputes.

It may be that the present writer exaggerates the importance of the arbitral handling of rights disputes in Australia. One authority (Professor Kingsley Laffer of Sydney University) advises that "most grievances are dealt with informally without the arbitration system being involved," and that "only the most difficult cases reach arbitration."

[29] The New South Wales Coal Industry Tribunal, in its state as well as in the federal jurisdiction, appears to take on minor disputes (on rights). It seems doubtful whether the Crown Employees Appeal Board handles such disputes. If it does not, it would seem probable that civil service employees in New South Wales do not have the benefit of arbitral service for their grievance controversies.

[30] South Australia's Public Service Arbitrator evidently is concerned primarily with disputes on interests, but it is possible that he also concerns himself with minor disputes. If not, it would not seem that the arbitration system in South Australia makes any provision for handling the grievances of state employees.

those two states. [31] Professor Kingsley Laffer suggests that the procedures of the wages boards for dealing with grievances are for the most part much less highly developed than is the case with the "strictly arbitral" tribunals. He thinks "it is fundamentally wrong to regard the wages boards as not part of the arbitral system." He points out that these boards largely follow the decisions of the arbitral jurisdictions (especially the Commonwealth), that "their chairmen make decisions (i.e., arbitrate compulsorily), that they deal with most of the same matters [and that] their differences in procedure are differences in degree rather than in kind."

THE DOCTRINES OF INTERSTATENESS AND OF AMBIT

So long as industrial disputes are interstate they are grist for Australian federal tribunals regardless of other differences. Any dispute over the rates of wages that are to be applicable to various classifications of workers (a controversy over interests), and any dispute over the alleged unwarrantable discharge of an individual employee (a controversy over rights), are appropriate matters for federal handling. But no industrial dispute, whether on interests or on rights, is properly a matter for such handling if it was not, as framed in the original log of claims, an interstate dispute. This important criterion of interstateness seems sometimes to go by the board. At any rate, "interim" claims to vary, if the original disputes were framed by logs of claims covering interstate disputes, may be dealt with by federal tribunals, even though intrastate. This can happen of course in the case of a dispute on interests, even in one over wage rates where the union claims increases for a large body of workers, all employed within a single state. For some reason, however, it seems especially likely to happen in the case of rights disputes. Such controversies—by and large being local, minor, or intraplant matters—would seem overwhelmingly likely to be *intrastate* rather than interstate in character, just as disputes on interests seem overwhelmingly likely to be genuinely interstate. It is no accident, apparently, that some of the most important of the recent industrial cases that have gone to the High Court have been matters in which that court concluded that the federal commissioner involved had wrongly taken jurisdiction over disputes that were really intrastate in character.[32]

---

[31] This writer does not know to what extent, if at all, the Tasmanian Public Service Tribunal concerns itself with grievance controversies. There is little question that it is concerned primarily, if not exclusively, with disputes on interests.

[32] See *The Queen v. Gough*, 17 *Industrial Information Bulletin* (hereafter cited as *IIB*) 1212; *The Queen v. Senior Commissioner*, 17 *IIB* 107; *The Queen v. Gallagher*, 18 *IIB* 633. Cited *infra*, pp. 77–79. These cases, held by the High Court to have arisen out of intrastate disputes, appear to have been rights-disputes matters. Apparently

As all the Australian systems presume the existence of organizations of employers and employees, there is, in fact, a high degree of interdependence between the arbitral tribunals and the industrial organizations. The tribunals, generally speaking, may be approached only by organizations.[33] Partly as a consequence of this interdependence there is also an uncommonly high degree of both worker and employer organization in Australia, the proportion of the gainfully employed industrial workers organized in trade unions evidently being more than twice that in the United States. Membership of Australian trade unions for 1963 was officially reported as 2,003,500, and the number of employed wage and salary earners (exclusive of "defense forces") in the same year as 3,314,600.[34] The trade union membership thus appears to be about 60 percent of gainfully employed workers.[35] For this country the *Statistical Abstract of the U.S., 1963,* p. 250, reports total membership of unions as 23.3 percent of employment in nonagricultural establishments. It appears that since 1963 the proportion of American trade unionists to all nonfarm workers has increased somewhat, with the number of cardholders running to 16,841,600 in 1964, an increase of about 255,000 over 1963. This figure still fell short of the peak of union membership of 17,490,000 in 1956. The high was 35.1 percent in 1954. Ten years later, in 1964, the proportion had dropped to 29.2 percent, as compared with 62 percent of the "total wage and salary earners" in Australia in 1962.[36]

As in this country, the federal writs run exclusively in the territories. The Australian systems date mostly from about the turn of the century. The Commonwealth Act (1904) was preceded by arbitration statutes in New South Wales, South Australia, and Western Australia, as well as by the Victorian wages-board legislation. The Tasmanian wages-board system and the Queensland arbitral arrangements developed some years later. Legislative overhauling in the states has been less fre-

---

they are beyond the power of federal tribunals both because they are intrastate and because dealing with them would involve such tribunals in the exercise of the judicial powers of the Commonwealth. It is insinuated in the text that interest-disputes cases also might be expected now and again to run afoul of the High Court because of their intrastateness, but this writer confesses that he can cite no such case.

[33] This seems to be true especially in the federal jurisdiction, although even there an individual may be a party. For example, an individual worker may be party applicant in a case involving cancellation of his registration. (See 92 *CAR* 89.)

[34] *Australia in Facts and Figures,* No. 84 (Australian News and Information Bureau, Department of the Interior, Canberra [1965]) at 28, 29.

[35] The *Industrial Information Bulletin* (Department of Labour & National Service, Canberra), reports on page 114 in its January, 1964, issue that in 1962 sixty-two percent of "total wage and salary earners" were members of unions. Sykes puts the percentage at 60. ("Labour Arbitration in Australia," 13 *American Journal of Comparative Law* 216 (1964) at 237.

[36] *Wall Street Journal,* September 21, 1965.

quent than in the federal system, the Commonwealth Arbitration Act having been amended no less than 39 times since 1904. While in the state jurisdictions industrial problems may be dealt with without a showing of the existence of disputes, the federal tribunals are constitutionally foreclosed from acting in their absence,[87] and from making awards unless there is an interstate industrial dispute between the parties. The federal Act defines 'an industrial dispute' as "(a) a dispute (including a threatened, impending or probable dispute) as to industrial matters which extends beyond the limits of any one state, and (b) a situation which is likely to give rise to a dispute as to industrial matters which so extends."[88] The High Court has commented on this requirement that there must be as a prerequisite "an industrial dispute, existing or impending": "This requirement," said the court, "can be satisfied by a 'paper-dispute' deliberately created . . . [which, however,] must be a real, not merely a fictitious, dispute. . . ."[39]

A dispute is "created" by filing of a "log of claims" by one party upon the other party, and the rejection of (or failure to reply to) those claims by that other party. If the claims are granted, by the respondent party or parties with resultant agreement, the Commission may formalize the accord by certifying the agreement which the parties have made, thereby giving it the effect of an award. The Commission may, however, refuse assent to a memorandum of agreement if it is of opinion that such certification would not be in the public interest. Usually, the Commission confronts not agreements but disputes about some or all of the working rules, and its task is to make awards over the conflicting claims of the parties. But, again, it may refrain from deciding any particular dispute if it believes that it would not be in the public interest to do so.

At regular intervals (at present it appears to be annually) the Commission in full bench, that is, in "presidential session," conducts a "Basic Wage Inquiry," fixing the basic wage, directly or indirectly, for all or nearly all federal awards. These full-bench basic-wage pro-

---

[87] But they are not so foreclosed in cases arising in the federal territories or in cases involving foreign trade. In the latter category the trade and commerce power gives a wider reach to the functioning of the federal tribunals.

[88] Conciliation and Arbitration Act, § 4. The concept of industrial dispute includes also such disputes in industries "carried on by, or under the control of, the Commonwealth" or any state, "whether or not the dispute extends beyond the limits of any one State. . . ." *Ibid.*

[89] The distinction between a "paper-dispute" which is "real" and one which is "fictitious" is not always clear. See The Queen v. Clth Arbitration Commission and ors, *ex parte* Printing Industry Employees' Union, per Windeyer, J., 19 *IIB* 239 (March 1964).

ceedings, although conventionally described as Basic Wage Inquiries, in reality are somewhat glorified proceedings to pass upon applications for award variations with respect to the basic wage incorporated in the Metal Trades Award.[40] Mr. Justice Foster explained these proceedings as follows:

> The Commission has no power to make an "inquiry" as such [i.e., unless there is a dispute]; it has a power and duty to settle interstate industrial disputes and must await the creation of such a dispute as defined in ... the Act. ... [These 1959 proceedings centered on] ... an application by the metal trades unions to vary an award made in 1958 in settlement of a dispute about the basic wage. ... [Other] unions were granted leave to join ... either as applicants for ... variation of [the basic wage rates in their respective awards] ... or as parties to ... new disputes about ... [basic wages]. The metal trades unions now, almost as a matter of tradition, start proceedings annually against their employers. ...[41]

Applications for changes or "variations" in the marginal wage rates for particular industries and callings, (and other award conditions, as well as rights disputes matters) are continually made to the Commission, typically constituted for this purpose by a single commissioner. But applications involving (1) alteration of the basic wage, (2) standard hours, or (3) long-service leave, must be dealt with by the Commission sitting as a bench of a least three presidential members.[42] Applications for new awards may come before individual commissioners, who prescribe the marginal and basic wage rates and the other conditions of employment that are to prevail in the industry, and incorporate the basic-wage rate ruling at the time the new award is made.

To sum up the principal statutory obligations, the Commission may not act unless (1) an industrial dispute has occurred or is likely to occur; (2) the dispute is industrial; (3) the dispute extends beyond the boundaries of any one state. Furthermore, even if the Commission finds

---

[40] The text of this important award in its original form (*Metal Trades Award*, 1952) appears at 73 *CAR* 325, at 413–477. (Print Nos. A 2459 and A 2460.) A more recent (consolidated) version of the award, as varied to October 31, 1960, after more than one hundred earlier variations, appears at 95 *CAR* 905–984 (Print No. A 9020), with citations to the earlier variations at pages 982–984. Professor Sykes reports that "there are 13,000 employer respondents" to this award. ("Labour Arbitration in Australia," 13 *American Journal of Comparative Law* 216 (1964) at 229.)

[41] Judgment, *Basic Wage Inquiry*, 1959, 91 *CAR* 706 (Print A 6618, p. 27). As has been noted, and as the Commission itself frequently has observed, its "... true function ... is to settle industrial disputes" (92 *CAR* 801). Although, as a rule, the tribunal does not think about these industrial disputes in the terms stressed in these pages as conflicts over rights and over interests, the dispute-settling function necessarily is dual, since, indubitably, such conflicts may erupt not only over what the rules are to be in future (*legislative* award-making and varying), but also over the judicial questions of what are the existing rights and obligations.

[42] Conciliation and Arbitration Act, 1904–1964, § 33. "Presidential members" are the president and deputy presidents, who are judges.

that a dispute exists or is likely to come into existence, that it is industrial, and finally, that it is interstate, the tribunal is limited in its
award-making power by the doctrine of "ambit." It may not make an
award whose terms would not lie within the span of union demands
on the high side and employer offers on the low. In other words, it may
not award a higher rate of wages than the highest rate demanded; nor
may it award a lower rate than the lowest rate offered by the employer.
These important doctrines of interstateness and of ambit are dealt
with more fully in the next chapter.

FEDERAL TRIBUNALS

The Commonwealth Industrial Court was created in 1956 and is
assigned the judicial, as opposed to the arbitral, functions in the Commonwealth system. It is constituted of not more than four judges of
which any two may exercise its jurisdiction.

The Public Service Arbitrator is a one-man tribunal, constituted
under the Public Service Arbitration Act, 1920–1956. The arbitrator
apparently is not required to be a lawyer or a judge.

The Coal Industry Tribunal is a one-judge authority created by the
terms of "twin" coal industry statutes of the Commonwealth and New
South Wales.[43] The Tribunal, as of June, 1965, is Mr. Justice F. H.
Gallagher, who is also a deputy president of the Commonwealth Conciliation and Arbitration Commission.

The Stevedoring Industry Authority is a tripartite tribunal whose
three members are appointed by the governor general. This agency is
not, like the Coal Tribunal, an award-making body. Awards in the
stevedoring industry, apparently, are made by the Commonwealth Conciliation and Arbitration Commission. The Authority's orders appear
to be of an administrative character, and they are appealable to the
Commission.[44]

The four types of ancillary tribunals previously referred to, particularly the tripartite or one-man boards of reference, the bipartite mine
conciliation committees, and the one-man local coal authorities, are
identified with disputes over changes in the terms of awards as well
as with controversies arising under those terms. However, they are
identified more with these latter, rights, disputes than are the five major

---

[43] Commonwealth Coal Industry Act, 1946–1956; New South Wales Coal Industry
Act, 1946–1951.
[44] The tribunal was created by the Stevedoring Industry Act, 1956–1962, § 10. In
one stevedoring industry case there is reference to a "variation or order of Stevedoring
Industry Commission" (92 CAR 5), but the Act does not mention any tribunal so
entitled.

tribunals,[45] although all of these, except possibly the Public Service Arbitrator, have something to do with such disputes. The chief concern of the Conciliation and Arbitration Commission, the Public Service Arbitrator, and the Coal Industry Tribunal is with the legislative business of making industrial awards in settlement of disputes on interests. The Industrial Court, naturally, is primarily concerned with rights disputes—especially interpretations.

The determinations of the federal Commission, whether in settlement of disputes on rights or on interests, are paramount in Australia. As Sir John Latham, former Chief Justice of the High Court, phrased it, "an award made by the Commonwealth Arbitration Court [now Commission] prevails over any inconsistent award or determination of any industrial tribunal and even over a law passed by a State Parliament." And Sir John added: "I doubt whether there is any parallel to this anywhere in the world."[46]

STATE TRIBUNALS

General Features

The Queensland apparatus, modified in 1961, is patterned closely upon the federal arrangements, with an Industrial Conciliation and Arbitration Commission for award-making and an Industrial Court for construing and applying award provisions.

Western Australia's major tribunals, as newly reconstituted in 1963, are the Industrial Commission, the Coal Industry Tribunal, and the Industrial Appeal Court, with boards of reference functioning in connection with the Commission and the Tribunal.[47] The Industrial Commission is the award-making tribunal. Its powers, however, seem to be less strictly limited to legislative matters than is the case with the Queensland Industrial Conciliation and Arbitration Commission. The Western Australian Industrial Appeal Court seems roughly to correspond to the Queensland Industrial Court.

In New South Wales, which is by far the most important, industrially, of the four arbitral states and whose arbitral arrangements will be most

---

[45] But this writer may be in error here. At any rate Professor Laffer notes that "Boards of Reference are largely legislative rather than rights tribunals," and adds that this is especially true of the Commonwealth boards.

[46] *The Industrial Power of the Commonwealth*, address before the Victorian Employers' Federation at Bendigo, Victoria, October 22, 1952 (pamphlet, n.d.). See Conciliation and Arbitration Act, 1904–1964, § 65. The principle involved seems analogous to the doctrine of federal pre-emption in the United States.

[47] The legislation which created the tripartite Western Australian Coal Industry Tribunal evidently continues on the books (Mining Act, 1904–1957). It provides for tripartite boards of reference which "have power to determine the industrial dispute, industrial matter or other matters and make an award therein." Section 321(b).

fully examined, the all-important Industrial Commission is an award-making and award-interpreting tribunal consisting entirely of judges[48] appointed by the governor. Authorities ancillary to the Commission, and authorized by the same legislation, are "not more than five" conciliation commissioners and a large number of important tripartite conciliation committees, severally identified with particular industries and responsible for more than half of New South Wales' awards. There is also a Coal Industry Tribunal (the agency referred to above in connection with the federal apparatus, a tribunal created by joint Commonwealth–New South Wales legislation to regulate and determine disputes in the coal industry) with its ancillary local coal authorities and mine conciliation committees already mentioned.

In South Australia the principal tribunal is the Industrial Court, although, as noted elsewhere, considerable use is made in this state of wages boards, now called industrial boards. The court in South Australia, like the New South Wales Industrial Commission, exercises both legislative (award-making) and judicial (award-interpreting) powers. The arbitral statute of South Australia, the Industrial Code, 1920–1963, was amended in December 1963 to provide for boards of reference.[49]

The arrangements in effect in the four arbitral states thus are similar to the federal pattern: their systems are compulsory; their tribunals are manned by persons not chosen by the parties, though some "fringe" tribunals are tripartite. An important difference is that the state tribunals may deal with industrial "matters" as well as disputes. And, of course, their jurisdiction is only intrastate.

The System in New South Wales

The state of New South Wales is the foremost industrial area in Australia, although the geographically much smaller state of Victoria is a close competitor. Its system of industrial arbitration, dating back to the 1890's, emerged even earlier than did that of the Commonwealth. For these reasons it seems appropriate to look in somewhat more detail at that system.

---

[48] The Industrial Arbitration Act, 1940–1959, specifies "not more than twelve persons." Section 14(1).

[49] Board-of-reference provisions are now beginning to appear in the awards of the South Australian Industrial Court. A recent example is that tribunal's award for "the industry of the occupations of persons employed in shops ... in the sale of goods in or about Port Pirie...." The board's functions include the "settlement of disputes on any matters arising out of this award." Clause 23. The text of the award was published in the *South Australian Government Gazette*, October 1, 1964, p. 1121.

According to Anderson, "The principal work of the [South Australian Industrial] Court is the making of industrial awards and the hearing of appeals against the determinations of [49] Industrial Boards." George Anderson, *Fixation of Wages in Australia* (Melbourne: 1929), p. 98.

That state's variety of compulsory industrial arbitration, as is pointed out by a leading Australian authority, "is not simply one of arbitration of disputes in industry [a field to which the Commonwealth jurisdiction is constitutionally limited]; that is only one facet of its operation. Its tribunals operate principally as authorities to determine the terms and conditions of employment generally in industry, and their decisions have the force and effect of law, subject only to the limitations which [the state] Parliament has imposed. . . . The system has broadened into a general one of industrial regulation, supported by numerous instances of direct parliamentary intervention and largely supplanting the process of collective bargaining. . . ."[50]

The apparatus of New South Wales, though elaborate, seems to be less complex than that of the Commonwealth. While the federal jurisdiction is dominated, as noted, by two tribunals, the Commonwealth Conciliation and Arbitration Commission and the relatively new Commonwealth Industrial Court, that of New South Wales is centered in, and chiefly governed by, a single tribunal, the Industrial Commission, a forum constituted entirely of judges.[51] The Commission exercises the functions which in the Commonwealth jurisdiction are divided between the Conciliation and Arbitration Commission and the Industrial Court.

The New South Wales Industrial Commission legislatively makes awards and judicially interprets and enforces them.[52] It is, of course, in connection with the exercise of these latter functions that it has occasion from time to time to deal with disputes on rights, an important example of which is detailed later on.[53]

The New South Wales Act also provides for conciliation commissioners, conciliation committees and apprenticeship councils (but makes no provision for boards of reference, at any rate by that name) . There are presently six conciliation commissioners in office, of whom two are identified as "apprenticeship commissioners." The others are assigned duties at large, which include service as chairmen of the many conciliation committees, with each committee made up of representatives of employers and employees in the industry (or industries) to which it is assigned.[54] Primarily, the commissioners, apart from their roles as committee chairmen, are concerned both with the "legislative" business of

---

[50] C. P. Mills (ed.), Nolan and Cohen's *Industrial Laws Annotated*, Book II, New South Wales (2nd ed.) at 57.

[51] Industrial Arbitration Act, 1940–1959, § 14.

[52] Its scope of action and authority seems nearly, if not quite, as wide as that of the Court of Arbitration of New Zealand.

[53] See the *Lima Crane* case, p. 101, *infra*.

[54] The *ex parte* committee members are appointed (upon recommendation of the Commission) by the "Minister of the Crown administering" the Act. The conciliation commissioners are appointed by the governor.

award making and amending ("varying"), and with grievance settlement, that is, with interests and with rights. And, be it noted, even the
business of award "variation," which is chiefly a process of interim legislating, may be utilized as an expedient (as it definitely is so utilized in
the federal jurisdiction) for effecting settlement of grievance-dispute
matters. The conciliation commissioners evidently spend a great deal
of time on grievances. The chief function of the important conciliation
committees appears to be the making of awards, subject to appeals to
the Commission. In addition, both the committees and the commissioners (acting individually) are authorized to summon parties to "compulsory conferences"—which circumstance suggests that the committees as
well as the individual commissioners may deal with "rights" disputes.[55]
Thus, apart from the apprenticeship councils with which we are not
concerned, it seems evident that all of the arbitral tribunals in New
South Wales (including the Coal Industry Tribunal discussed below)
act to some degree on rights disputes.

The authority which the New South Wales Act has conferred upon
the conciliation committees, wide as it is, seems not to include the kind
of authority exercised by the boards of reference in the Commonwealth
and in Western Australia. The terms of the statute both confirm this
conclusion and disclose awareness on the part of the legislature of the
existence and complementary functions of private, intraplant organizations. The section reads: "A [conciliation] committee shall, as far as is
consistent with the maintenance of industrial peace, deal only with the
wages and hours of employment, leaving all other matters to shop committees, industrial councils, or voluntary committees formed for the
purpose of adjusting the industrial relationship of employer and employee. A member of . . . the [Industrial] Commission may act as the
chairman of any industrial council."[56]

---

[55] Industrial Arbitration Act, 1940–1959, § 25(1), (3); § 77C. Section 20 provides that
the conciliation committee "shall have . . . power to inquire into any industrial matter
in the industry or calling for which it is established, and in respect of such industry . . .
may . . . make an order or award . . . determining any industrial matter." Apparently,
an applicant for an award or a variation of an award has a right to apply either to
the Industrial Commission—all judges—or to the appropriate conciliation committee
(tripartite and constituted wholly or in the major part of laymen) for determination
of the matter. Professor Laffer points out that the committees are responsible for
more than half of the state awards in New South Wales. He notes, further, that the
calling of compulsory conferences by the conciliation commissioners achieves results
similar to those attained in other jurisdictions by resort to boards of reference.

[56] Industrial Arbitration Act, 1940–1959, § 23. But it seems to happen only rarely.
At any rate a well-informed federal judge (Mr. Justice John Moore, member of the
Commonwealth Conciliation and Arbitration Commission) comments on Section 23:
". . . I know of only one case of an industrial council being established and for all
practical purposes the section can as far as I am aware be ignored." (Letter to this
writer, dated May 14, 1963.)

The Industrial Commission itself, while it is mostly occupied with the settlement of major disputes on interests by the award-making process, has some authority and responsibility in respect to minor disputes. The statute provides that it ". . . shall have the powers and may exercise the jurisdiction hereby conferred on . . . conciliation committees . . . and may exercise the powers, jurisdiction and functions of a conciliation committee in respect of any industry or calling. . . ."[57] Professor Laffer points out that the work of the New South Wales Industrial Commission (as is true of the Australian tribunals generally) "is residual, dealing with matters, whether on rights or on interests, on which the parties cannot agree." He stresses the fact that in the New South Wales and other Australian tribunals most grievances are dealt with informally.

It should be emphasized that in New South Wales the arbitral machinery must act upon the differences not only over what the parties' rights and duties shall be *in the future* (herein called "interest disputes"), but also over what are their rights and duties *as of now* (herein called "rights disputes"). In the federal sphere, on the contrary, the Commonwealth Commission, as has been noted, is precluded (as a matter of law) from exercising the judicial power of the Commonwealth. That power (to deal with rights disputes) is vested in the Commonwealth Industrial Court. Thus the business of interpretation of award clauses, although beyond the power of the federal Commission, is fully within the jurisdiction of the Commonwealth and the New South Wales Industrial Commission. That Commission—definitely a court—legislates, but judicially, to make working rules for the future; it determines, also judicially, disputes over job tenure—most importantly dismissal cases—which may, and do, also come before the Commonwealth Industrial Court and the Commonwealth Arbitration Commission, as well as before the state tribunals. Most of these rights disputes seem to involve single individual workers or very small groups of employees. There seems to be little question that applications are made to the federal Commission to settle grievance disputes (as to job tenure, etc.) in face of the hazard that in order to deal with them the Commission may in the end be resolving what actually is an *intrastate* dispute, and possibly one running beyond the allowable ambit.

The Industrial Commission of New South Wales and the conciliation commissioners and committees deal with these two significantly different classes of labor disputes—those on rights and those on interests. But

---

[57] Industrial Arbitration Act, 1940–1959, § 30. There appears to be extensive mutual sharing of powers between the Commission and the conciliation committees, which latter wield important powers also exercised by the Commission, among them the power to make and vary industrial awards. *Ibid.,* §§ 20–22.

the state awards, like the federal instruments, are unlikely to contain provisions (similar to the grievance procedures characteristic of American labor contracts) for the handling of grievances or other minor differences. As Professor Sykes points out, "there is an almost total lack [in Australia] of anything like the [American] grievance procedure. . . ."[58] Grievance disputes seem to give less trouble when they arise between parties to state awards than when they develop between parties to federal determinations. In the latter situation it would seem to be illegal for state tribunals to touch them, although they probably could cope more effectively with these local disputes than the federal tribunals which often face embarrassing dilemmas arising out of questions of interstateness (and perhaps even questions of ambit).

The foregoing summary of the New South Wales system of industrial arbitration gives some indication of that state's central apparatus for labor-dispute settlement—viz. the structure of conciliation committees, apprenticeship councils, conciliation commissioners, and at the summit the Industrial Commission. Though no more than an outline, the tracing of its contours has disclosed, perhaps inevitably, that the legislatively arbitral business of award-making is shared by the Commission (award-maker in chief) with the very important conciliation commissioners and, still more, with the tripartite conciliation committees.[59] What is not so obvious is the fact that the Commission (which is nothing if not judicial) devotes much attention to the adjudication of disputes on rights, and that this task also is shared by the conciliation commissioners and apparently also by the conciliation committees.

The System in Queensland

In Queensland a new set of tribunals was established in 1961 by a statute which repealed the earlier legislation. The Industrial Conciliation and Arbitration Act of 1961 followed the pattern set in the Commonwealth jurisdiction in 1956. The 1961 law created a one-judge Industrial Court to exercise judicial functions and an Industrial Conciliation and Arbitration Commission (composed of not more than five persons) whose function is legislative (i.e., arbitral).[60] The ancillary system of industrial magistrates who exercise judicial and (contingent) arbitral powers, is retained. An informed Australian writer, Professor

---

[58] Sykes, *op. cit.* (n.40 *supra*), p. 233.
[59] But subject to appeal to the Commission.
[60] A full bench of the Commission is made up of not less than three commissioners. The industrial court for the purpose of handling appeals from the Commission is constituted by the court's president-judge and two members of the Conciliation and Arbitration Commission. When so constituted it is known as the "Full Industrial Court."

E. I. Sykes of the University of Queensland, points out that although the industrial magistrates have powers of conciliation, they do not have authority to arbitrate except in matters "remitted to them for determination by the Commission."[61]

The System in South Australia

The chief tribunal in South Australia is the Industrial Court. That tribunal, however, is not limited to the exercise of judicial functions as are the similarly named bodies in the Commonwealth, Queensland, and Western Australia. Like the New South Wales Industrial Commission, it exercises legislative (i.e. award-making) as well as judicial powers. It is a one-man body constituted of a president-judge.[62] There are also widely used tripartite industrial boards (formerly called wages boards) assigned to the various industries for which they make determinations; there is also a Board of Industry, made up of the president of the Industrial Court and four commissioners, which from time to time declares the basic or "living wage." The Industrial Court "delivers awards concerning workers who do not come under the jurisdiction of [any of] the Industrial Boards and hears appeals from decisions of [those] Boards."[63] In 1961 the South Australian State legislature enacted the Public Service Arbitration Act, providing for a Public Service Arbitrator.

The System in Western Australia

In 1963 the State Parliament of Western Australia extensively revised its industrial legislation, bringing it more nearly into line with the federal pattern.[64] The new statute replaced the previous tripartite Court of Arbitration with an award-making Industrial Commission made up of four lay comissioners. In addition to its award-making powers, the Commission may make interpertations of, and enforce, its agreements

---

[61] "The New Arbitration Act in Queensland," *The Journal of Industrial Relations* (Sydney), III, 143 (October, 1961) at 145. Professor Sykes points out that the New Industrial Court "has both an original and an appellate jurisdiction in judicial matters." The court is empowered to make interpretations of the Act and of awards made under it. (The Act, § 8(9).) It hears the "graver industrial offenses," with charges of breach of award going in most cases to the industrial magistrates. Sykes, *op. cit.,* p. 144. The role of these magistrates seems to be chiefly one of award enforcement. They appear to be most widely used in Western Australia, Queensland, and New South Wales.

[62] The president, we are told, "may be joined by two assessors [or *ex parte* members] employed in the industry concerned." Deputy presidents may also be appointed. Commonwealth Bureau of Census and Statistics, *Labour Report,* 1961, at 49.

[63] *Ibid.*

[64] Industrial Arbitration Act, 1912–1963. For an authoritative resume of the 1963 revisions in the Western Australian system, see D. W. Oxnam's "Recent Changes in the Western Australian System," *The Journal of Industrial Relations* (Sydney), VI (July, 1964), p. 84.

and awards;[65] but it may not impose penalties, power for which is reserved to an appeal court and the industrial magistrates. The new statute also created the three-judge Industrial Appeal Court.[66] The Western Australian Coal Industry Tribunal, a five-man tripartite award-making authority, has been continued in power. Boards of reference are provided for by the new statute (as they were in the old) for awards in industry generally. The Mining Act[67] remains on the books with its provisions for boards of reference for coal and, apparently, other mining operations.

Arrangements in Coal Mining in New South Wales and Queensland

The foregoing pages have been devoted to the arbitral arrangements for industry at large in some of the arbitral states, especially in New South Wales, with passing reference to Western Australian mining legislation and to provisions made there for coal mining boards of reference. There remains for special consideration the important industry of coal mining in New South Wales and Queensland, where that industry bulks larger than it does on the western coast.

The problem of effecting workable accommodation between industrial situations and political arrangements is often extremely difficult, especially in countries like Australia and the United States, marked by the often troublesome federal–state jurisdiction pattern. The problem is a formidable one in Australian coal mining. As one Australian writer points out:

> Coal mining is a matter which falls within State jurisdiction, but the supply of coal is obviously a matter of vital national concern. Accordingly the (Clth) *Coal Industry Act 1946–1956* and parallel New South Wales legislation provided for the establishment under Commonwealth and New South Wales auspices of a Joint Coal Board, and through it the assumption of a measure of Commonwealth responsibility for the production of New South Wales coal and its distribution throughout Australia. . . .[68]

The dominant arbitral agency in coal mining in Eastern Australia is the Coal Industry Tribunal constituted by one man, a judge, and established under the twin statutes. The tribunal is empowered "to consider and determine interstate disputes, and in respect of New South Wales only, intra-State disputes between the Australian Coal and Shale Em-

---

[65] Industrial Arbitration Act, 1912–1963, § 90(1)(a).

[66] *Id.*, Sections 108A and 108B.

[67] Mining Act, 1904–1957 (Board of Reference, Section 321(1)(b)).

[68] Ross Anderson, "The States and Relations with the Commonwealth," Chapter IV in *Essays on the Australian Constitution* (Rae Else-Mitchell, ed., Sydney: Law Book Co. of Australasia, 2nd ed. 1961), p. 111.

ployees' Federation and employers in the coal mining industry."[69] The twin statutes incorporate a common preamble:

Whereas it has been agreed between the governments of the Commonwealth of Australia and of the State of New South Wales that they shall take measures for securing and maintaining adequate supplies of coal to meet the needs for that commodity throughout Australia and in trade with other countries, and for providing for the regulation and improvement of the coal industry in the State of New South Wales and for other matters relating to the production, supply and distribution of coal. . . .

The Commonwealth Industrial Court has held that the power over intrastate disputes in coal mining, assigned to the tribunal under Section 34 (1)(a) of the Commonwealth Coal Industry Act, "falls within the Commonwealth's legislative power with respect to conciliation and arbitration (Sec. 51) (xxxv) of the Constitution."[70] Section 44 of the (Commonwealth) Act provides:

An award, order or determination of the Tribunal or a decision of a Local Coal Authority under this Act shall not be challenged, appealed against, quashed or called into question, or be subject to prohibition, mandamus or injunction, in any court on any account whatever.[71]

The Coal Industry Act also provides for two classes of ancillary agencies functioning locally at particular mines. These agencies, and especially the mine conciliation committees, evidently carry out functions similar to those exercised by boards of reference. These subordinate agencies are: local coal authorities made up of one or several persons, and (bipartite) mine conciliation committees. The committees are authorized "to deal with all industrial grievances arising at the coal mine . . . and to refer to a Local Coal Authority any dispute as to which the committee cannot agree. . . ."[72]

---

[69] *Labour Report,* 1961, at 47. The twin statutes are: Commonwealth Coal Industry Act, 1946–1956, and New South Wales Coal Industry Act, 1946–1951. This evidently means that the tribunal has power to decide interstate disputes in the coal mining industry between the Coal and Shale Employees Federation (or any other union in the industry?) and employers in the industry. The powers of the tribunal are set out in identical language, Section 34(1) of the Commonwealth, Section 40(1) of the New South Wales Act, Sections designed, as are the whole of the twin statutes, to operate side by side. The subsections clothe the tribunal with power to consider and determine:
(a) an industrial dispute extending beyond the limits of any one state
(b) an industrial dispute in the state
(c) an industrial matter arising under an award or order of the [Commonwealth Arbitration] Court or of the tribunal relating to the coal mining industry of the state . . .
(d) an industrial dispute or matter referred to the tribunal by a local coal authority.
[70] NSW Combined Colliery Proprietors Ass'n v. Australian Coal and Shale Employees Federation. *Federal Law Reports* 72 (May, 1957) at 77.
[71] The same language appears in Section 50 of the New South Wales Coal Industry Act, 1946–1951.
[72] Commonwealth Act, § 43(a)(c); New South Wales Act, § 49(a)(c).

Local Coal Authorities

These tribunals are composed of a person or persons appointed by the Coal Industry Tribunal to be such authorities. Section 43A of the state statute provides in subsection (1) that "[w]hen exercising its powers . . . in relation to a dispute or matter not affecting members of the [Coal and Shale Employees] Federation (other than members excepted by the [Joint Coal] Board . . .), the Local Coal Authority is to consist of a person appointed to be a Local Coal Authority, as Chairman, and two or three other members representative of employers and the same number of other members representative of employees, . . . selected by the Chairman, according to the subject matter to be dealt with, from among persons appointed by the Tribunal. . . ."[73] These tripartite (or one-man) authorities are empowered to hear and settle local industrial disputes in the industry, including ". . . any dispute referred . . . by a (bipartite) Mine Conciliation Committee."[74] The Supreme Court of New South Wales has commented on the functions of local coal authorities. One of these functions, that court observed, "is judicial in the same sense that the function of a strict court is judicial."[75] The local coal authority for New South Wales had been challenged in that court as to its right to order the reinstatement of a certain deputy at the Nebo Colliery. The court concluded that the authority lacked power to make such an order, inasmuch as it "would not be an award, order or determination in settlement of a dispute as to an industrial matter."[76] The court went on to comment on the powers of these authorities: "[W]ith respect to a local industrial matter," the court said, "the powers of the Local Coal Authority are wide and general. . . . [T]he legislature has conferred upon it the power to settle on the spot any dispute likely to affect amicable employer-employee relations. . . ."[77]

Mine Conciliation Committees

The (bipartite) mine conciliation committees are made up of persons (equally representative of the management of the mine and of union mine workers), appointed, upon the Tribunal's request, by the Joint

---

[73] Commonwealth Act, § 37A(1); New South Wales Act, § 43A(1). Apart from the somewhat ambiguous statutory language, this writer notes that in some of the cases under the twin statutes the local coal authorities are referred to as one-man bodies. See, for example, the *Dobb* case, p. 60 *infra*.

[74] New South Wales Coal Industry Act, 1946–1951, § 44.

[75] Ex parte Australian Iron and Steel, Ltd., re John Dobb *and* Illawarra Deputies, etc., 12 *IIB* (December 10, 1957) at 1142. Supreme Court of New South Wales: Judgment October 12, 1957; Reasons, December 12, 1957. Appealed to High Court. Appeal dismissed, *sub nom* Australian Iron and Steel, Ltd., v. Dobb and ano. 90 *CLR* 586.

[76] *Dobb* case in High Court 90 *CLR* 586. See *infra* p. 60.

[77] *Ibid.*

Coal Board. Their functions are "to deal with all industrial grievances arising at the coal mine . . . ," "to endeavour by conciliation to maintain harmonious relations between . . . [management and workers]" and "to refer to a Local Coal Authority any dispute as to which the Committee cannot agree. . . ."[78] These committees, thus empowered by the joint statutes to deal with "all industrial grievances" arising at the coal mines, may fairly be considered as, in effect, boards of reference for the coal mining industry. Their functions, however, seem to be somewhat more extensive than those of the boards of reference inasmuch as the committees are charged "to endeavour by conciliation to maintain harmonious relations. . . ."[79]

In summary, it appears that the mine conciliation committees devote themselves exclusively to conciliation while the local coal authorities are arbitral tribunals.

The Commonwealth Coal Reference Board for Queensland

It has been remarked that the Industrial Arbitration Act of New South Wales makes no provision for boards of reference; neither do the Commonwealth–New South Wales "twin" coal statutes. Yet it is evident that this Commonwealth coal statute has been construed and applied in a fashion permitting incorporation, in some coal industry awards, of provisions for boards of reference and the establishment of such boards. Some of these awards also incorporate "disputes" clauses for good measure.[80]

One of the earliest of the coal mining awards was the *Coal Mining Industry (Miners) Award, 1954, Queensland*. That award contains both board-of-reference and disputes clauses.[81] A tripartite board was constituted by the Tribunal and carried on actively over a considerable period

---

[78] Commonwealth statute (Coal Industry Act, 1946–1956), § 43(a); New South Wales statute (Coal Industry Act, 1946–1951), § 49(a). The wording of the clause is identical in the two statutes.

[79] Commonwealth Act, § 43; State Act, § 49.

[80] Board-of-reference provisions are included in the *Coal Mining Industry (Miners) Award, 1954, Queensland* (CR 1057). Other Coal Tribunal awards probably include such provisions. Among them are: *Coal Mining Industry (Engine Drviers' and Firemen's Award, 1952* (Coal Reference Board, 902); *Coal Mining Industry (Electrical and Engineering Trades) Award, 1954, Queensland* (CR 1063); *Collieries Staff Award, 1956, Queensland* (CR 1189).

Some of the awards which incorporate board-of-reference clauses also include "disputes" clauses, which provide that: "In the event of any dispute arising as to the interpretation of [the] . . . award . . . , and not amicably settled, . . . it shall be referred to the appropriate industrial authority." See also *Coal Mining Industry (Miners) Award, 1954, Queensland, cl. 22(c)*.

[81] Board of Reference, clause 21; Disputes, clause 22. Under clause 21, the board has the function, *inter alia*, of ". . . settlement of disputes arising out of any of the terms . . ." of the award. Under clause 22 ". . . any dispute arising as to the interpretation of this award . . . shall be referred to the appropriate industrial authority."

period of years and apparently continues to function. It evidently operates under authority of the board-of-reference provisions not only of the Miners Award just mentioned but also under the sanctions of several other coal mining awards for Queensland.[82]

THE LEGISLATIVE TASK OF THE AUSTRALIAN TRIBUNALS

The great task to which the Australian apparatus is primarily devoted is the legislative one of making working rules—mostly as to wage rates— for the future.[83] In the United States that work is done jointly by representatives of employers and employees in collective bargaining, rather than by judges or legislators. Minor or even major segments of these working rules, Down Under, may be made by bargaining before any tribunal is approached; more substantial but still minor parts of them are made after the tribunals have had their say (i.e., over-award wages). In this country fag ends that have successfully resisted negotiatory treatment, even with wet-nursing by a federal or state conciliator, may be passed on to lay arbitrators who would much prefer to be left at peace with their grievance cases. In both countries orderly rule-making— whether by "legislative" arbitration on interests (in Australia), by "judicial" arbitration on rights (in America), or by privately legislative collective bargaining on interests (in America and to a small degree in Australia)—may be supplanted by disorderly strike or other direct action.

In Australia the "arbitral" process has emerged as a legislative one albeit presided over by judges, whereas in this country the "arbitral" process gradually has assumed the form of a judicial procedure presided over by laymen. One result of this contrasting evolution is the semantic paradox that in Australia the word "arbitration" connotes, primarily, third-party determination of labor disputes over divergent interests, whereas in this country it connotes primarily third-party determination of labor disputes over controverted rights. In both countries the arbitral process is one of third-party determination.[84] But it is also a process which is applied to one class of disputes in Australia and to an entirely different class of disputes in this country—to disputes about what the

---

[82] This tripartite board was made up of a chairman appointed by the Coal Industry Tribunal (under authority of Section 50, Conciliation and Arbitration Act, 1904–1964, and Commonwealth Coal Industry Act, 1946–1956), and representative members evidently nominated *ex parte* from case to case. Thus, in effect, it is as many boards as there are awards, or sets of parties, involved in its different cases.

[83] One Australian writer observes that the industrial legislation "was meant to prevent strikes rather than to regulate wages." But he adds that "in practice, the arbitration courts found that very soon they had to deal with wage regulation." G. V. Portus, *Australia: An Economic Interpretation* (2nd ed., Sydney, 1933) at 79.

[84] In American dictionaries the process is defined as third-party determination *by a person agreed upon by the parties.*

working rules are to be in the future, and to disputes about what the working rules mean and how they are to be given effect in particular situations, respectively. Moreover, it is important to note also that while in Autsralia the third-party "determiners" are public officials (largely judges), in America they are private (largely lay) persons.[85]

Finally, it must be emphasized that the federal Arbitration Commission may not legally arbitrate disputes over rights, because for it to do that would involve the exercise of "some part of the judicial power of the Commonwealth." The same thing must be said about the powers of (federal) boards of reference to be considered presently. But it seems to be true, nevertheless, that both the Commission and the boards do sometimes determine disputes on rights.

The Australian system, as Professor Laffer notes, "covers both interests and grievances." It manages, in practice, to provide for the determination of industrial disputes, whether they arise out of grievances (i.e., rights disputes) or out of interest conflicts, such as those about rates of wages. The rationale of the system with respect to disputes of the latter type is clear enough. It is with regard to disputes over rights that one has the greatest difficulty. Perhaps it may be best understood by Americans if considered in the context of a concrete case dealt with by the method of award variation. This method is a commonplace one in interest-dispute situations wherein one of the parties applies for a variation in the wage rate provided for in an existing award. If the application is granted, the tribunal will make an award varying the principal award in terms of the application.

The same procedure may be resorted to in disputes over rights. The illustrative case is a dispute (No. 430 of 1963, about certain conditions of employment among wharf clerks) which arose in 1963 between parties to *The Clerks (Shipping) Award, 1948*, which in turn had emerged from another dispute, or series of disputes (No. 470 of 1947). Both disputes came before the Commonwealth Conciliation and Arbitration Commission. The earlier dispute or disputes, out of which the award

---

[85] On this point Professor Laffer comments: ". . . you appear to be wrongly contrasting the Australian and the U. S. systems. The difference is rather that the Australian . . . system covers both interests and grievances [i.e., rights] while the American system is confined largely to the latter. Confusion probably arises from the heavy reliance on informal grievance procedures in Australia, the arbitration system being more of a backstop." But this writer is bound to say that he questions whether in Australia there is "heavy reliance on informal grievance procedures."

Professor D. C. Thomson of the Law School of the University of Sydney remarks that ". . . by contrast with the position in North America, there is, in this country, no really developed system to deal with disputes arising out of the operation of awards" (in a review of C. P. Mills' "Federal Industrial Law," in the *Journal of Industrial Relations* (Sydney) October, 1963, at 167).

emerged, and possibly also the 1963 dispute "arising under" the award, were interstate.[86] The 1963 application for variation arose "from a dispute about the dismissal of three employees by the Darling Island Stevedoring & Lighterage Co. Ltd. ..."[87] This dispute the present writer deems to be a controversy over rights. Upon application by the Oversea Shipping Representatives Association, of which the Lighterage Company was a member, the matter came before Comissioner Findlay in Sydney on September 2, 1963, and again before the same commissioner on September 13 in Canberra. After investigation and hearing "it was found the Company was justified in terminating the services of the three clerks. ..." At the same time the applicant Association "was advised to apply for a variation of the award [in terms of the application] to provide suitable machinery to hear charges ... [of] ... misconduct in the course of ... [employment]."[88] Despite the opposition of the respondent Federated Clerks Union of Australia, the Commission "ordered and prescribed" an elaborate, 7-paragraph variation in the award, designed, *inter alia,* to cope with dismissal situations.[89] Presumably these procedures are for disputes "hereafter arising" rather than for Dispute No. 430 of 1963, since, as noted above, "it was found [without recourse to the procedures, that] the Company was justified. ..." Thus the current dispute before the Commission evidently was determined by its decision which also varied the award by prescription of a kind of grievance procedure for use in disputes "hereafter arising." The current dispute thus was decided by a simple arbitral finding of justification. However, similar disputes in the future presumably will be determined by the "grievance procedures" provided by the award variation.[90]

COLLECTIVE BARGAINING IN AUSTRALIA

It would be a mistake to assume that the Australian conciliative and arbitral processes function in total absence of collective bargaining. As the president of the Commonwealth Commission has expressed it, bar-

[86] The 1963 dispute is reported in Print No. A 9241 which is the source of this writer's information about the case. The award, dated April 30, 1948, as previously varied February 20, 1956, was published at 84 *CAR* 290. Print No. A 9241 throws no light on the nature of the dispute or disputes which gave rise to the original award.
[87] Print No. A 9241, at 1. The reason for the dismissal was said to have been the failure of the employees to report on time after a teabreak.
[88] *Ibid.*
[89] *Ibid.,* pp. 2, 3.
[90] Consideration of the *Shipping Clerks* case naturally suggests the question: How would such a dismissal case be dealt with in absence of an award covering the parties? This writer does not know, although he fancies it would be by application to the court. And he queries: Could a party (absent an award) file an application, citing a dispute about the dismissals? If so, could the Commission "find" justification—or lack of it? If the latter, would an "order" emerge, and could the employees be reinstated? Presumably the answer is "yes" in each case.

gaining and arbitration coexist.[91] The collective bargaining that goes on before and after arbitration in Australia is fundamentally the same process that we know in America. A difference of some moment, no doubt, is the circumstance that Down Under the bargaining process is much less likely to be carried forward by the principals on their own initiative than is the case in this country, and it seems to require the guidance of a conciliator or a commissioner. This, to an observer, is especially true of such bargaining as takes place before arbitration. The postarbitral over-award bargaining is more self-generating—and also, perhaps, more likely to be punctuated by strike action than is the case with any prearbitral bargaining that may take place. In prearbitral bargaining the parties may often agree on everything but one or two major issues.

Although neither preliminary nor postliminary negotiations appear to be widespread, there is no doubt that over-award payments are ubiquitous. Indeed, it seems to be true that in recent years such wage payments have been growing at a faster rate than have award wages. But it is uncertain to what extent they are negotiated. This writer's guess is that they are less generally negotiated than unilaterally determined by employers.[92] However, it may well be true that this writer has underestimated the extent of collective bargaining in Australia. Professor Laffer, for one, suggests that the amount of it "is by no means trifling."

It is probable that (although there is not a little postarbitral negotiating for over-award rates) the bulk of the wage bargaining in Australia is a *pre*arbitral process. Consent awards certainly are numerous, and they reflect, at the least, assisted negotiation. There evidently is very little entirely independent prearbitral negotiating done in Australia, and the likely explanation is that both unions and employers are conditioned to "approaching" tribunals instead of each other with their problems. This seems to be the case both with respect to the negotiation of new codes of rules covering wage rates, hours, and "conditions" and, even more strikingly, with regard to grievances and other rights disputes. One reason for the reliance on tribunals for the settlement of rights disputes lies in the fact that it is only the rarest of awards—"con-

---

[91] Sir Richard Kirby, "Some Comparisons between Compulsory Arbitration and Collective Bargaining," 7 *Journal of Industrial Relations*, 1–17 (March, 1965).
[92] "Negotiations concerning over-award payments are at present largely informal, and are frequently on an individual basis." Kingsley Laffer, "The Australian Economy, September 1960," 36 *The Economic Record* 449, 455 (December, 1960). Professor Laffer comments in a note to this writer: "Post-arbitral bargaining can often scarcely be called 'collective bargaining.' A market rate for a particular type of work gets established, sometimes through industrial pressure, and then tends to be paid to individuals without much bargaining."

sent" or otherwise—that contains clauses to govern the handling of grievances. The nearest approach that is at all common is the device of boards of reference. These boards are charged with "the settlement of disputes on any matters arising out of" awards. Thus they appear to have responsibility for disputes on interests as well as those on rights, although their concern seems to be mostly the latter.

Both negotiation of new codes and the settlement of rights disputes are initiated by the joint response of the disputing parties to the summons from the commissioner to a compulsory conference. Such conferences are the opening gambits in the arbitral process, whether the claiming party (usually a union) seeks a wage increase for its member-employees, or the reinstatement of a member allegedly discharged without just cause, thus precipitating in the first case a dispute on interests, and in the second, one on rights. This writer has had the privilege of sitting in on several compulsory conferences, and he has been greatly impressed by the skill and patience with which these federal conciliators and commissioners deal with the very tough situations which they must handle. What goes on at these conferences is skillfully assisted collective bargaining.

In the measure that the negotiations succeed, an "industrial agreement" (or part of it) will result. This accord may be converted by the tribunal into a "consent award." Such consent awards may be worked out also after the disputes have been "referred into arbitration" in default of agreement in conference. But, failing agreement "the Commission shall . . . [by arbitration] determine the dispute."[93]

Consent awards seem to be less numerous than those determined arbitrally by the tribunal, but it is surprising that there are as many such awards as there are. Not infrequently some clauses—less often all of them—will be agreed upon by the time the commissioner decides that there is no more "give" in the situation and refers the dispute into arbitration.

In New South Wales the tripartite conciliation committees (ancillary to the Industrial Commission), like the federal commissioners and conciliators, seem to be no less mediating than award-making tribunals. It is quite clear that it is expected that conciliation (assisted bargaining) will go on—and it evidently does go on—before the committees. The committee chairman[94] is the active conciliating influence on the committee, as is definitely suggested by the language of the statute:

---

[93] Conciliation and Arbitration Act, 1904–1964, § 32.

[94] One of the five conciliation commissioners provided for in the statute. The conciliation commissioners, however, are not members of the Industrial Commission.

... it shall be the duty of the chairman to endeavour to bring the parties to an agreement, and ... the committee shall ... carefully inquire into [the matters in dispute and] ... the chairman may ... do all such things as he deems right and proper for inducing the parties to come to a fair and amicable settlement. ...[95]

---

[95] The Industrial Arbitration Act, 1940–1959 (New South Wales), § 77B. The statute provides that "where the votes for and against any matter are equal the chairman shall decide. ..." Section 77E(b).

Chapter 3
Effects of Doctrines of Interstateness and Ambit on Arbitration Functions

ARBITRATION IN AUSTRALIA AND IN AMERICA

The systems of arbitration currently operational in Australia and in this country are so different, procedurally and substantively, that one wonders that the same word can do duty as a label for both. The word "arbitration" Down Under refers to the Australian (and New Zealand) systems of courtlike public tribunals called industrial commissions or courts before which the process of arbitration goes forward. That process is the "legislative" one of determining (after default of the parties in reaching agreement by negotiation with or without the aid of conciliation) what working rules are to govern the industrial relations of the parties during a specified period of years for the future. Such determinations here in the United States are typically made by a process that is known to us as "collective bargaining." The process in Australia is a publicly legislative one—it *is* arbitration.[1] Our process is privately legislative—it is *not* arbitration. Both processes center on conflicting interests and the formulation of procedures for their reconciliation. The process which is dominant in Australia is chiefly distinguishable from the one which goes on at bargaining sessions and in legislatures by the circumstance that its *procedure* is judicial—characterized by the hearing of parties, the calling of evidence by witnesses, and so forth. Our collective bargaining is anything but judicial. It closely resembles, in procedure and in substance, the public legislative process, but it is a private process engaged in by private groups representing the disputing organizations.

More important than it might seem at first blush is the semantic fact (quite understandable in view of the sharp procedural differences between them) that the two processes of formulating industrial working rules, the Australian and the American, so alike in purpose, are called by such different names.

---

[1] Professor Kingsley Laffer cautions that "a good deal of arbitral work in Australia is done fairly informally, i.e., by a judge in a private conference or by a commissioner in conciliating a dispute at a factory."

44

We have stated above that the Australian system was devised, so to say, for a legislative purpose. Yet, in the Australian context putting it so is misleading, because for several years after the setting up of the arbitral machinery at the turn of the century, the tribunals evidently were assumed to have a judicial function.[2] At the outset, the agencies were indubitably courts, at least in the sense of trappings and procedures. Their business was to make codes or working rules, called "awards," which may be directly compared with the working rules constantly being ground out by negotiation rather than governmental prescription in labor-contract proceedings in the United States. In due course the High Court came to recognize that what the major tribunals were doing was legislating—but legislating judicially.

The arbitral tribunals soon found themselves confronted with industrial disputes, not over the conflicting interests of the parties in the effectuation of rule changes (mostly rules as to wages), but with disputes about what the existing award clauses meant, and how they should be applied and enforced. It was natural that the award-making tribunals (mostly dominated by judges) should take on also the judicial business of award interpretation, application, and enforcement. True, they were law-making rather than adjudicating bodies, but they made their laws through nonparliamentary procedures—by judicial process.

In the *Boilermaker's* case the Australian High Court reached the conclusion that the Conciliation and Arbitration Commission (which until then had been the Court of Conciliation and Arbitration) could not constitutionally exercise the judicial power of the Commonwealth.[3] In consonance with this judgment the Commonwealth Parliament in 1956 created the Commonwealth Industrial Court. The result is that,

---

[2] "... the term 'arbitration' connotes a judicial tribunal by whatever name it is called.... Otherwise the members of the tribunal would not be judicial persons at all, but dictators or lawgivers exercising the power of legislation, not of adjudication." *Australian Boot Trade Employees Federation* and *Whybrow and Co.*, 10 *CLR* 266, 280. But in the next quarter-century the pendulum was to swing full circle. In 1935 a member of the arbitration court, Drake-Brockman, J., observed: "It is the principal duty of this Court to prevent and settle industrial disputes. The Court is only in a minor degree a Court of Law. Its legal judicial functions are practically limited to the interpretation and enforcement of its own awards. [When, in 1956, the "Court" became the "Commission," even these powers were withdrawn and assigned to the newly created Commonwealth Industrial Court.] Its main activities [those of the Commission] are directed to the making of awards which is normally a legislative function...." *Railways* case, 34 *CAR* 15.

Professor Mills observes that "it is not always true ... [that the interpretation of awards] involves the exercise of judicial power; it is only when it is sought to make that interpretation binding on [the] parties ... that it attracts this principle...."

[3] Attorney General for Australia v. The Queen, The Privy Council, London (1957) A.C. 288; The Queen v. Kirby, 94 *CLR* 254 (1956). To the new "Commission" was granted "only nonjudicial powers, mainly arbitral...." Commonwealth Industrial Court, in Australian Iron & Steel, Ltd. v. Australasian Coal and Shale Employees Federation, 1 *Fed. Law Reports*, 54, at 65 (April 18, 1957).

in the terminology used in these pages, the Commission now deals primarily with disputes on interests and the newly created court chiefly with disputes over rights. The former "arbitrates," *making* awards; the latter adjudicates, *interpreting* awards. Thus the court does mainly what in this country is done by our private arbitrators in determining disputes on rights. The Industrial Court may not "arbitrate" in the Australian sense, though it does so in the American sense; it never legislates, although carrying on in a country where most of the industrial tribunals do just that. Thus in the Commonwealth jurisdiction, the arbitral dispute-settlement procedures are those presided over by the Arbitration Commission (and by other federal award-making tribunals like the Public Service Arbitrator) in the resolution of disputes over interests—disputes settled here mostly by private negotiations.

In two of the four "arbitral" states—Queensland and Western Australia—the pattern is substantially the same as in the Commonwealth. But since the states are not bound by the constitutional limitations upon the Commonwealth (as laid down in the Boilermaker's case), the new Industrial Commission in Western Australia may interpret awards as well as make them, and this, probably, is the case also in Queensland. In New South Wales and South Australia the major tribunals settle disputes over rights as well as those over interests, adjudicating as well as legislating.

The foregoing comparative recital seems to suggest (as a simplified scheme, and apart from the relatively insignificant amount of Australian collective bargaining) the assignment of the adjudication of industrial rights disputes to the industrial courts in Australia, to the army of private arbitrators in America, and to the regular courts in both countries. It further suggests the assignment of interest disputes to the other Australian tribunals and to private bargaining groups and public conciliators in the United States.

It is important to note that there is a growing tendency for the states, which also promulgate basic wages, intrastate, to follow closely, or adopt outright, the Commonwealth basic wage as prescribed from time to time by the federal Commission. The most recent movement in this direction is reflected in a determination made by the Western Australian Industrial Commission fixing the basic wage for that state at £15/8/-, a figure identical with the federal rate for Perth and representing an increase of 3½ shillings. The new rate, in contrast to the previous practice in Western Australia of fixing different basic-wage rates for different parts of the state, applies throughout the state.[4]

---

[4] *The West Australian*, September 23, 1964.

INTERSTATENESS

The most important difference in dispute settlement between federal and state jurisdictions—and certainly the most significant one in the present context—is that federal tribunals are constitutionally precluded from dealing with any industrial disputes except those "extending beyond the limits of any one State."[5] Federal awards must have "interstateness." State awards, presumably, must be free from it. The state tribunals, in other words, are free from such federal constitutional inhibitions as limit the jurisdiction of the Commonwealth bodies. The latter, as noted, may not act unless they find (1) that there is a dispute, (2) that it is industrial, and (3) that it is interstate. The state tribunals, most important of all, are free from the obligation to limit themselves to *dispute* situations. They are free to deal with industrial *matters,* even though those matters do not involve disputes.

The distinction as to "interstateness" between Commonwealth and state jurisdictions has crucial significance with regard to disputes on rights. These disputes tend to be local—and thus very likely intrastate. Authentic interstate grievance disputes can and do exist, although they are probably rare.

When a dispute "arises under" an award, the odds are that partly because it does "arise under," it may be intrastate and perhaps susceptible to handling *de novo* by a state tribunal, although, as will be noted, also legitimately to be dealt with by a federal tribunal. Such a dispute is grist for federal action and the parties will be likely to resolve doubts in favor of "interstateness." Understandably they may prefer to have the matter considered by the federal commissioner who made the award initially. In these circumstances the federal commissioner may well take jurisdiction. One well-known lay commentator in Australia writes as follows on this problem of interstateness:

... the principle was established that any industry, even though its operations were confined to the limits of a country town, might enjoy a dispute extending beyond the limits of one State, provided that the workers in the industry made common cause with their fellow workers across the border. The workers in many industries have done this with alacrity, for it may happen that they will get from the Commonwealth tribunal what they have failed to get from their State Court or ... Wages Board. In this way has originated the Australian system of a dual regulation of industry, and the Australian game of 'playing off one against the other.' Capital and labour have learnt to fight a flying battle of

---

[5] The Australian Constitution in Section 51 (xxxv) provides: "The Parliament shall ... have power to make laws ... with respect to: ... Conciliation and arbitration for the prevention and settlement of industrial disputes extending beyond the limits of any one State."

legal shifts and dodges, chasing each other from court to court, elaborating a harassing tactic of quibble and obstructiveness and evasion. The spectacle of these maneuvres is unique; one can see nothing quite like it in any other country of the world.[6]

Interstateness, as has been intimated, is much more likely to be an attribute of interest disputes than it is of those over rights. If the minor dispute does not arise under a Commonwealth award previously made, it is almost certain not to be a dispute over which a federal tribunal would be constitutionally justified in assuming jurisdiction, although if it happened to erupt near a state boundary and not all of the disputants were in the same state, it might warrantably attract the jurisdiction of a Commonwealth tribunal.

If the minor dispute arises under an existing Commonwealth award, or is between parties to such an award, it may or may not constitutionally furnish justification for a federal arbitral tribunal to assume jurisdiction over it. Such justification would depend on whether it was, or was not, in the words of Mr. Justice J. C. Moore, "a matter which had been part of the original interstate . . . dispute which properly enabled the Commission to make the original Federal award. . . ."[7] His Honour's comments refer to the *Cairns Meat Export Company [Gough]* case, in which the High Court decided that the Cairns Meat Export Company action in dismissing four employees (although company and employees were bound by the Commonwealth Meat Industry Award) could not be dealt with by the Commonwealth Conciliation and Arbitration Commission, the dispute arising, (at least two years after the making of the original award) from the dismissal of the four men, not having been within the ambit of the award made in settlement of the original dispute and not being an interstate matter.[8]

---

[6] W. K. Hancock, *Australia* (Sydney: Australasian Publishing Co., 1931), p. 99. But one can see something very similar in the United States, where a similar, dual, federal-state system of governmental agencies not unnaturally has produced similar results.

[7] Letter to this writer dated May 14, 1963, commenting on *The Queen v. Gough*. That case arose out of a dispute under the *Federal Meat Industry Award* 1959 (93 *CAR* 660–693); it is dealt with in some detail as the *Cairns* case in the text below. The case before the Commonwealth Commission is in 17 *IIB* 870, 996. The High Court's judgment is in 17 *IIB* 1212 (November 1962), and in 36 *Australian Law Journal* 249 (Dec. 28, 1962). The company was one of nearly one hundred respondents in the case.

[8] In the *Gough* case, the High Court considered that the commissioner's ". . . real authority was to settle any industrial dispute extending beyond any one State, but the matter was not of that character. . . ." 17 *IIB* at 1215. But note the comment of the Commonwealth industrial registrar (letter to this writer dated October 21, 1965): "If the original log of claims be one extending . . . [etc.] and an award is made on this dispute, then it is considered that a claim for a variation to the award as to something in one State only comes within the original log and as such the Commission is empowered to vary its award."

For another case of the same type see: *The Queen v. The Senior Commissioner* (The Tramways case) 17 *IIB* 407 (May, 1962), involving The Melbourne Tramways (Interim) Award. See also 17 *IIB* 211.

As Mr. Justice Moore points out, the *Cairns Meat* case and the *Melbourne Tramways* case dramatize the crucial problem incident to efforts made by federal arbitral tribunals to deal with localized minor disputes. "Even though," as he suggests, federal arbitrators "have always been conscious of this jurisdictional problem, quite a number of minor matters [actually intrastate, and probably disputes on rights] are, in fact, dealt with by members of the Commission and are not challenged in the High Court." His Honour continues: "But when an employer (or a union) disagrees sufficiently strongly with a decision . . . there is always the possibility that it will go to the High Court and have the action of the Commission prohibited. . . . [G]enerally speaking . . . both unions and employers are prepared to allow a Federal Commissioner to deal with local matters. . . ."[9] Indeed, if these local matters are not thus realistically (even if not quite constitutionally) dealt with by the federal tribunals they may go by default—unsettled except perhaps by direct action.

Interstateness and "local" Disputes

This important and essential concept of interstateness, in the context of a pluralistic political system and parallel state and federal systems of arbitration, can lead to serious difficulties in practice. A detour to consider them may be in order. The state arbitral tribunals, of course, are free from headaches about "disputes extending," although, given a desire to avoid the federal jurisdiction, these interstate disputes no doubt could be dealt with by a series of separate state determinations. The state tribunals are better adapted, inasmuch as their jurisdictions are more local, to deal with rights disputes as well as with intrastate disputes over interests. And there is no question that they can, and do, render important service in this respect. About ninety percent of Australia's industrial workers are covered by either state or federal arbitral tribunals, about half of the country's workers being covered by federal awards. Where intraplant industrial disputes develop there would seem to be no serious problem if the disputants are covered by a state award. Similarly there would seem to be no serious problem in the case of local "industrial troubles" involving disputants covered by Commonwealth awards—to the extent that, as Mr. Justice Moore puts it, "both unions and employers are prepared to allow a Federal Commissioner to deal with local matters," at least as long as the Commonwealth arbitral authorities are, realistically, disposed to meet the parties half way, and the parties are willing to forego their rights to appeal.

---

[9] Mr. Justice Moore, in a letter to this writer, dated May 14, 1963.

Naturally, a persistent multiplication of challenges (in the High Court) to the jurisdiction of the federal arbitral authority in course of time might well render that authority helpless to deal with minor disputes. Presumably, if the parties to minor disputes happen to be subject to federal awards and the federal tribunals do not assume jurisdiction, those disputes may go by default because the state tribunals, presumably, may not trespass upon federal jurisdiction. The federal agencies may not act because the local controversies, although disputes "arising under," are not "disputes extending." The state tribunals may not act because they are precluded from infringement upon federal award jurisdiction. Or may they? The parties in the rare local disputes in which they are not covered by awards, either federal or state, would seem to be in less serious straits than local disputants covered by federal awards, where the federal arbitrators, for whatever reason, are strict constructionists, refusing to take jurisdiction in the absence of a "dispute extending." Parties to intraplant disputes would seem unlikely to be at a loss for official arbitral attention if they are covered by state awards. Nor are disputants involved in intraplant disputes in industries or callings not covered by any award, state or federal, because in all probability they will be in a position successfully to attract the jurisdiction of a state tribunal to settle their disputes. The really neglected ones would appear to be the disputants, engaged in intrastate disputes, who are covered by federal awards—unless they have the luck to have assigned to their dispute a federal commissioner who is satisfied that they really are engaged in an interstate dispute. Otherwise the disputants so situated would seem to be in a bad way. One wonders whether a state tribunal may come to their aid. This foreign observer is confused. He is perplexed about the ways and means found—if ways and means *were* found—for settlement of the disputes which the federal commissioner was not permitted to settle, for example in the *Cairns Meat* and *Melbourne Tramways* cases. And what happens to the parties to an intraplant dispute who are bound by a federal award, yet now must be denied access to a federal commissioner because he is satisfied at the outset that he lacks jurisdiction because their interim dispute is merely intraplant?

This vexing problem is commented on by Professor Laffer: "The State tribunals could act in all cases of intra-plant grievances under federal awards other than strict rights disputes, in which cases they cannot usurp the jurisdiction of the Commonwealth Industrial Court. This is not really an important issue, practically, in Australia, though there are special cases like the ones you cite [i.e., *The Queen v. The*

Senior Commissioner (the Tramways case, 17 IIB 4077].... If this did become a very important issue either the State tribunals would enter this field ... or, alternatively, the Commonwealth would find ways of ensuring that ... [such disputes] could legally be dealt with by Commonwealth tribunals...."

Sir Richard Kirby, the president of the Commonwealth Conciliation and Arbitration Commission, as pointed out by Professor Laffer, has discussed these jurisdictional difficulties in his most recent annual report.[10] Such difficulties arise, Sir Richard observes, "... when stoppages the subject of ... [referral to the Commission] occur or are threatened in a single undertaking ... although the employers and employees of the undertaking and the work concerned are covered by the Commission's Awards.... These stoppages ... are generally of the sudden 'flare up' variety.... The dispute may be over the dismissal ... of an employee.... Such disputes generally require the intervention of a third party ... although the dispute is a local one.... But ... [because of the parties'] urgent need the Commissioner on many occasions is asked by them to give his services when in law he may have no jurisdiction to decide the dispute. The Commissioner's task ... is on those occasions extremely difficult.... The obvious difficulty is that the type of dispute concerned ... is generally not a dispute extending ... beyond the limits of any one State, whereas the Commission's jurisdiction ... is restricted to disputes ... which do so extend...."[11]

The president goes on to suggest a procedure which he considers calculated to enable the Commission properly to take jurisdiction over these local, rights-disputes cases. It seems best to quote his language without attempt at much condensation:

A party about to serve a log of claims in ... an interstate dispute could include a demand that, in the event of a future dispute arising in any one or more undertakings covered by the Award (whether those undertakings were in one state or not) between parties bound by the Award made in settlement of the original dispute, ... the future dispute so arising should be settled by ... the Commission in the same way as industrial disputes as defined in the ... [federal] Act may be settled.... If such a demand were refused, particular disputes arising subsequently to the making of the Award could ... be properly regarded as part of the original interstate dispute ... notwithstanding the facts that they arose subsequently to the making of the Award and that they themselves did not extend beyond one State. The party making such a demand could ... require additionally that some internal grievance procedure should ... [first be followed].'"[12]

---

[10] Eighth Annual Report of the President of the ... Commission ... for the period August 14, 1963 to August 13, 1964, p. 7.
[11] *Id.*, pp. 7, 8.
[12] *Id.*, p. 8.

The concept of "interstateness," of course, is a familiar one in this country. Here, however, the key word is "commerce," defined in the National Labor Relations Act as amended by the *Labor-Management Relations Act, 1947,* as meaning "trade ... or communication among the several States ...," with an additional phrase, "affecting commerce," defined as meaning "... burdening or obstructing commerce ... or tending to lead to a labor dispute burdening ... commerce or the free flow of commerce."[13]

AMBIT

There is another limitation upon arbitral functions (though relevant especially to disputes over interests), namely that of ambit. It stems in Australia partly from constitutional limitations, but it is inherent in the very nature of labor disputes everywhere—affecting, therefore, both Australian and American arbitrators, whether state or federal and whether public or private. No experienced arbitrator in this country, even though he is under no constitutional restraint, would think it proper to make an award prescribing higher wage rates than the highest rates demanded or lower rates than the lowest rates offered. The Australian arbitrator is constitutionally forbidden to decide more than the case before him.

The concept of ambit rests upon the proposition that the terms prescribed in awards must lie within the area between the lowest terms offered and the highest ones demanded. The award, in short, must be "within ambit." As put by the late Justice A. W. Foster of the federal Commission, applications by unions "for variations in their basic wage can continue to be made until the ambit of their original claim is reached, but then a new 'dispute' must be created if ... [further] variations are desired."[14]

When the federal Arbitration Commission is dealing with an application to vary an award, the order of variation, therefore, must fall within the ambit framed by the log of demands and the responsive counterlog, which together laid the foundation for the original award. Strictly speaking, there seems no good reason why questions of ambit and interstateness should be entangled, although naturally both may arise in the same proceeding. Whether interim disputes—those arising

---

[13] National Labor Relations Act as amended by the *Labor-Management Relations (Taft-Hartley) Act, 1947,* § 2. The words in the text are defined in implementation and clarification of the "purpose and policy" of the LMRA "to prescribe the legitimate rights of both employees and employers in their relations affecting commerce ... and to protect the rights of the public in connection with labor disputes affecting commerce." LMRA, § 1.

[14] Judgment, *Basic Wage Inquiry,* 1959 (Print A 6618) 91 *CAR* 680, at 706.

under an award previously made—must conform to the requirement of interstateness is a question as to which the Australian authorities differ:

1) The Commonwealth Industrial Registrar: "A claim for a variation to the award *as to something in one State only* comes within the original log and as such the Commission is empowered to . . . vary . . . [it]."[15]
2) The High Court: "[The Commissioner's] . . . real authority [as in the *Gough* case, arising under the Federal Meat Industry Award] was to settle any industrial dispute extending beyond any one State, but the matter [of the dismissal of four men] was not of that character."[16]

It may be found in award-variation cases that what is demanded is something that may not be awarded because it is not within ambit, or because the interim dispute is not interstate. But, as to interstateness, at least, the question seems unsettled. If ambit is lacking or if the interim dispute is intrastate, the arbitrator may have a two-fold basis for dismissal of the application. However, as the determination made must settle the dispute,[17] and a settlement will not result if an application is dismissed, Australian federal arbitrators must be extremely reluctant to dismiss, thus frustrating the prime purpose of the system.

Many years ago the High Court said (per Dixon, J.): The Arbitration Court (now the Commission) ". . . can make no award except . . . for the purpose of settling . . . a dispute. The terms of the award must therefore be relevant to the dispute or its settlement. . . . In a dispute about wages the parties by their demands . . . may define the greatest amount claimed, on the one hand, or on the other hand, the amount conceded. . . . The award . . . cannot be outside these limits. It must be relevant [i.e., within ambit]; and it is relevant neither to the dispute nor to its settlement to prescribe a wage lower than that conceded or higher than that demanded. This principle applies not merely to the initial award but also to its subsequent variation. . . ."[18] In a much more recent case before the Conciliation and Arbitration Commission—evidently an application to vary an award—Commissioner Donovan commented that since "the current award rates are considerably below those originally claimed, ambit still exists. . . ."[19]

---

[15] Letter to this writer, dated October 21, 1965, from Mr. A. E. O'Brien, industrial registrar, Commonwealth of Australia. (Emphasis added.)
[16] *Gough* case (Cairns Meat Export Co.) 17 *IIB* at 1215; *Australian Law Journal*, December 28, 1962, p. 249.
[17] "The basic wage which this Commission fixes must settle the dispute. . . ." Foster, J. in Judgment, *Basic Wage Inquiry*, 1959 (Print No. A 6618) 91 *CAR* 680, at 107.
[18] Australian Tramway Employees Association *and* the Commissioner for Road Transport (N.S.W.) 53 *CLR* 90, at 103. The High Court also held in the *Whybrow* case that the arbitration court "could not award a higher rate than had been demanded." 11 *CLR* 1 (1910).
[19] *Builders' Labourers Award*, 1962. Complaints Nos. 1233 and 1234 of 1964. Print No. B 244, p. 3.

The problem of ambit is less simple in disputes about non-wage matters than it is in disputes over wage rates. A distinguished Australian authority has pointed out that "[o]n the whole, the test of the question whether the award made is within the 'ambit' of a dispute seems to be whether . . . [it] is 'relevant to the disagreement or dispute and legally appropriate for its settlement.' "[20]

---

[20] R. M. Eggleston, "Industrial Relations," Chapter VIII in *Essays on the Australian Constitution* (Rae Else-Mitchell, ed., Sydney: Law Book Co. of Australasia, 2nd ed. 1961), p. 227.

Chapter 4

Labor Disputes on Rights and on Interests

The Making and Interpreting of Rules

The settlement of minor, or grievance, disputes in Australia generally relates not to hoped-for changes in existing rates, or in the schedules or hours of work—changes with which the Australian arbitral systems are chiefly concerned—but to the meaning and application of *existing* rules as to rates, hours, and conditions. The central concern of the Australian tribunals is to determine what changes, if any, shall be made in the existing rules, rather than to make decisions about what the rules mean or how they should be applied and enforced.

These disputes over meanings, it is to be noted, are controversies which, at least on theory, are arbitrally determined in processes which culminate in *decisions* on disputed rights. An example is a controversy (Dispute No. 589 of 1959) about the "employment of a certain overseer," decided by a Commonwealth commissioner.[1] In contrast to these rights disputes cases are those over interests, which are also arbitrally determined in processes culminating in *awards*. An example of such a dispute is Case No. 822 of 1959, a controversy about overtime and other matters decided by another commissioner.[2] The italicised headnotes in the first class of disputes run, typically: "Industrial dispute . . . decision issued"; in the second class, they run: "Industrial dispute . . . award made." Australian awards may fairly be thought of as a special (legislative) type of decision, viz. one involving disputes over interests and dispositive of questions as to what rates of wages, or other working rules, are to bind the parties in the future; all other decisions (which are judicial rather than legislative) resolve disputes over the present rights and obligations of the parties. These latter, also settled by the arbitral process, are the central concern of this monograph.

The Commonwealth Conciliation and Arbitration Act, 1904–1964, defines an "industrial dispute" as "a dispute (including a threatened,

---

[1] Federated Engine Drivers *and* Department of Public Works, Tasmania, 92 *CAR* 10. "Decision issued." It is these "decisions," perhaps nonarbitral yet reached by arbitral process, around which semantic ambiguities seem to cluster.
[2] The Australian Workers Union v. the Canberra Steam Laundry, 92 *CAR* 714. "Award made."

impending, or probable dispute) as to industrial matters . . . and a situation which is likely to give rise to a dispute as to . . ." such matters.[3]
Certainly a grievance matter at the shop level, and no less certainly
many of the questions which arise about wage rates, job tenure, and
so forth, whether they are disputes "arising under" awards or arising
in "award-free" shops, are matters which come within the statutory
language, broadly construed. They are "likely to give rise to a dispute
as to industrial matters," if indeed such a dispute has not already
erupted.

The distinction between "interest" disputes over the making of the
rules, and "rights" disputes over their interpretation and application
seems not to be widely recognized in Australia under that terminology.
But Australian scholars seem aware of it. Thus Edward I. Sykes, Professor of Law at the University of Queensland and a highly respected
student of industrial relations in Australia, writes:

> The distinction between the situation where the parties wish the court to
> prescribe general rules of a legislative nature and that where what they want is
> an *ad hoc* settlement of an actual dispute is a very real one which is constantly
> brought out by the activities of the Australian arbitral bodies.[4]

Apart from some uncertainty over Professor Sykes' apparent implication that the determination of "general rules of a legislative nature" do
not involve "actual disputes,"[5] it seems clear that he has in mind the
distinction which this writer endeavors to draw between disputes on
"rights" and those on "interests." Whatever the terminology, as Sykes
points out, "there is no doubt that the boundary line is sometimes very
difficult to draw."

Another well-known Australian authority on industrial relations,
Professor Kingsley Laffer of the University of Sydney, points out that,

> . . . we do not normally make a sharp distinction between interest disputes
> and rights disputes; indeed this distinction is largely unknown in Australia.
> Arbitrators [here] commonly go ahead and settle disputes of all kinds, in some
> cases even to the extent of varying the awards, if this seems expedient. . . .[6]

Both kinds of disputes are "actual," both are real. "Grievance" disputes on rights may be said to stem, indirectly, from "contract" dis-

---

[3] Commonwealth Conciliation and Arbitration Act, 1904–1964, § 4.
[4] Edward I. Sykes, "Labour Regulation by Courts: The Australian Experience," 52 *Northwestern University Law Review* 462 (September–October, 1957) at 477.
[5] Even "where the parties wish the Court to prescribe general rules of a legislative nature," it would seem that there must be "an actual dispute"—at least in the Commonwealth jurisdiction. Otherwise the arbitral tribunal could not be approached!
[6] Kingsley M. Laffer, "The Working of Australian Compulsory Arbitration," (address at the Industrial Relations Conference, University of Hawaii, Honolulu, April 23, 1962), in Roberts and Brissenden (eds.) *The Challenge of Industrial Relations in the Pacific-Asian Countries* (Honolulu: East-West Center Press), 59, p. 64.

putes on interests, turning as they typically do on the meaning or application of award (or contract) terms previously prescribed or agreed to. The latter, resolved by the techniques of negotiation, legislation, or arbitration Australian style—all looking to the determination of working rules for the future—confer rights and impose duties with respect to the relation of employment. They are disputes over what the parties' respective rights are to be during a limited future period. But during that period questions inevitably arise about the meaning and application of the rules, however formulated, and these derivative questions in turn must be resolved. The resolution of both classes of disputes, those incident to efforts to *make* the rules and those arising out of their administration, may be effected by arbitration.

The rights–interests dichotomy in the settlement of industrial disputes transcends geography; it is implicit in the settlement process both here and in Australia. The dichotomy significantly affects procedures and shapes and limits contracts and awards in both countries. It therefore seems desirable to look closely at this dualism.[7]

Disputes over rights are controversies arising out of differences regarding the interpretation or application of rules already in effect. These established rules variously are codified in individual or collective agreements (whether written or oral), in awards, in statutes, or even in the accepted practices or customs of the plant or industry.

The fundamental and distinguishing characteristic of an "interest" dispute would seem to be, that, in respect to it, neither party may base its demands on any existing contractual, statutory or "custom-made" prerogative or right. Neither party is under any duty to accept the other party's proposals, or to enter into an agreement. The position of each party is based, not upon any claim of right, but upon what it considers necessary or desirable for the protection or promotion of what it conceives to be its own best interest. A dispute of this kind reflects the conflicting economic or social interests of the parties and embodies considerations of policy. The resolution of a dispute of this sort (whether by direct action, negotiation, legislation or arbitration) results in the establishment of new rights. When such a dispute is dealt with arbitrally, the arbitrator must deal not with legal rights but with the conflicting views of the parties as to their respective interests, goals or desires. The arbitrator's task centers, not upon a calculus of legal rights and duties, but upon social, ethical and economic criteria; in sum, upon matters of policy.

---

[7] For an early discussion of this aspect of labor-dispute settlement, see Spielmans, "Labor Disputes on Rights and on Interests" 29 *American Economic Review* (1939), p. 299.

ADJUDICATION OR ARBITRATION?

When the New South Wales Industrial Commission (or any of the Australian arbitral tribunals) interprets, applies, or enforces existing awards, it simply construes or gives effect to their terms, so protecting the *rights* of the parties. When one or both of the parties approach the Commission with applications for sets of rules to constitute new awards to govern their future industrial relations, or with requests for changes in the rules by variation of the original awards, the tribunal is legislating in (or against) the *interests* of one or both the parties, declaring or changing the law accordingly. In rights disputes the tribunal applies existing law—it adjudicates; in interest disputes it makes new law— it legislates. The settlement of rights disputes requires exercise of judicial power, that of disputes on interests the use of legislative power. As expressed by a distinguished authority, "judicial power requires the application to a particular dispute of a pre-existing legal norm."[8]

There has been not a little controversy in Australia as to the nature of arbitral and judicial power and process. It has been argued in the Australian courts that arbitration is, and that it is not, a judicial function. The prevailing judicial position is that the making of industrial awards in settlement of disputes is not a judicial but is an arbitral or legislative function.[9] Much more recently, in consonance with the prevailing view in *Alexander's* case, the High Court held that non-judicial power, such as the power to arbitrate, may not be vested in federal courts.[10] This decision recognizes the converse proposition that judicial power may not be vested in Commonwealth award-making tribunals. But nothing of all this has application intrastate in New South Wales where the Industrial Commission legislates and adjudicates, *ad lib*, untroubled by concern about its authority to preside over the forwarding of both processes. Indeed, it appears that none of the Australian state constitutions makes any distinction between judicial

---

[8] Geoffrey Sawer (Professor of Law at the Australian National University, Canberra), "Judicial Power under the Constitution," Chapter III in *Essays on the Australian Constitution* (Rae Else-Mitchell, ed., Sydney: Law Book Co. of Australasia, 2nd ed. 1961), p. 74.

[9] High Court of Australia in *Alexander's* case (1918) 25 *Commonwealth Law Reports* 434. There were vigorous dissents by Griffith, C. J. and Barton, J., who supported what apparently had been the prevalent views up to that time, that industrial arbitration was judicial in character. Nature of function turns on nature of dispute.

[10] *Boilermaker's* case: *The Queen v. Kirby* (1957) Appeal Cases 288; 95 *CLR* 529. It was held in this case that such a tribunal as the Commonwealth Conciliation and Arbitration Commission, charged with the exercise of nonjudicial (i.e. arbitral or legislative) powers, may not also exercise any part of the judicial power of the Commonwealth. Following on this epochal decision the Commonwealth Parliament established the Commonwealth Industrial Court to exercise the judicial power.

and nonjudicial functions, although the legislatures of Queensland and Western Australia have deliberately chosen to follow the pattern of the federal legislation of 1956, which compelled separation of functions in the Commonwealth jurisdiction.

THE CALCULUS OF RIGHTS AND INTERESTS

In some respects the dichotomy implied in the classification of labor disputes into those respectively over rights and over interests is an unreal one. Certainly not all dispute cases fall neatly into these slots. It seems—at any rate to this writer—less difficult in this country than it is Down Under definitely to identify particular disputes as belonging, naturally, to one or the other of the two categories. The American arbitrator usually confronts a question or questions as to the meaning or application of particular clauses of a collective bargaining agreement. These questions clearly bear upon the rights (and/or duties) of the parties to that agreement, under its terms. If the agreement specifies a particular rate for a lathe operator, an employee, John Doe, who is a qualified lathe operator and does that work has a right to that rate. If he does not get it he may become the focus of a dispute over the recognition and enforcement of that right. The same lathe hand may also have an interest in getting a rate higher than that specified in the agreement, and his fellow workers typically have similar interests in getting, if they can, rates for their several classifications that are higher than the current "rightful" rates respectively assigned to them. If they demand these higher job rates and are refused them, the whole group of employees is likely to become claimants in a dispute. The American arbitrator usually deals with disputes involving matters specified in the agreement. When employees, having failed to win from their employer consent to the higher job rates, come to the arbitrator (after he has made an award in the minor rights dispute requiring the employer to pay John Doe the contract rate) and request that he arbitrate their major, interest, dispute about raising the whole set of job rates, the arbitrator is likely to feel that he is operating outside of his usual role. If he underakes the assignment he may expose himself to the criticism that he is changing his function from that of a private judge, construing and applying, to that of a law-maker—criticism which carries with it the damning insinuation that he is contributing to the promotion of judge-made law.

Although the dichotomy of types of industrial disputes (rights and interests) is not generally recognized in Australia, its significance has not gone unnoticed. Two cases are now presented, *The Dobb Case* and

The Farthing Case which illustrate the distinction between labor disputes on rights and on interests.

The Dobb Case involves a local coal authority and the Supreme Court of New South Wales (under the Coal Industry Act, 1946). In this case John Dobb, who was the Local Coal Authority for the Southern District, was a respondent.[11] The case centered upon an application by Australian Iron and Steel, Ltd., to restrain Dobb [the "Authority"] and the Association [i.e., the Union] "from proceeding further in an application . . . for the reinstatement [by 'an award, order or determination of that Authority] of one . . . Hunt . . . [as] Deputy at the Nebo Colliery." Hunt evidently had been discharged or "stood down." The merits of the application are of no moment here. But some of the comments made by the judges on the nature of judicial powers seem relevant. Some reference already has been made to the machinery provided for dealing with rights disputes in the coal mining industry.[12]

One of the functions of the local coal authority, according to the New South Wales Supreme Court's judgment in the Dobb case, "is judicial in the same sense that the function of a strict court is judicial, in that its determination may impose an obligation upon, or affect the rights of, the parties to the dispute."[13] The court goes on to point out that under the National Security (Coal Control) Regulations, local reference boards had been set up "with power 'to settle disputes as to any matters likely to affect the amicable relations of employers and employees in the coal mining industry.' "[14] The court observed that the legislature had "conferred upon it [i.e. upon Dobb as the Local Coal Authority] the power to settle on the spot any dispute likely to affect amicable employer-employee relations. . . ."[15] Obviously, either disputes on rights or those on interests may "affect amicable employer-employee relations." The court, further, pointed out that it had been argued that a tribunal was free to deal only "with some right established by some earlier award or, possibly, by industrial agreement, or by contract or statute." The court said ". . . that you must first find a right given by such an award [as a right is given similarly by an American labor contract] and the only power given to the [Coal Industry] tribunal was to deal with breaches of such a right."[16] The Supreme

---

[11] *Ex parte* Australian Iron and Steel, Ltd., re John Dobb [the Local Coal Authority] and Illawarra Deputies and Shot Firers' Association. Judgment, Dec. 2, 1957. Reasons, Dec. 12, 1957 (12 *IIB* 1142, December, 1957). The respondent company appealed to the High Court, which dismissed the appeal. (98 *CLR* 586).

[12] See above at pp. 34–38.

[13] *Dobb* case, n.11, *supra,* and 12 *IIB* at 1143.

[14] *Ibid.*

[15] *Id.*, at 1145.

[16] Citing *Rawson's* case. 1921 *Arbitration Reports* (N.S.W.) 138.

Court in the Dobb case pointed out that in the New South Wales Coal Industry Act, 1946–1951, the legislature of New South Wales gave jurisdiction not only to the Coal Industry Tribunal, but also to the local coal authorities over disputes involving "the right to dismiss or to refuse to employ, or the duty to reinstate in employment, a particular person or class of persons."[17] The court supported the reinstatement application, although in doing so it implied that reinstatements conferred new rights, and therefore that disputes about them were interest disputes.[18]

In the course of his dissenting opinion, Owen, J., paraphrasing the argument of counsel for the Local Coal Authority (Dobb), refers to a "distinction . . . drawn between 'decisions' of a Local [Coal] Authority and 'awards' of the [Coal Industry] Tribunal." His Honour proceeded to a discussion of duties under awards and the bearing of such duties upon disputes on interests and on rights. The Coal Industry Tribunal, he suggested, ". . . might make an 'award' directing the reinstatement of an employee and thereby impose a duty [thus settling a dispute on interests] in which case a Local Coal Authority [Dobb] would have jurisdiction to deal with a dispute [on rights] arising from the nonperformance of the duty thus imposed." It was argued by counsel, His Honour noted, "that a Local Coal Authority could order the reinstatement of an employee [even] where no pre-existing duty to reinstate existed . . . ; that . . . [the] Authority had jurisdiction to create such a duty [so settling a dispute over interests] whether its order creating it was called an 'award' or a 'decision.' "[19]

The Farthing Case is presented to further illustrate the distinction between labor disputes on rights and on interests. This discharge case, referred to a Commonwealth Board of Reference, affected an employee covered by the (Commonwealth) *Meat Industry (Shops and Small Goods Factories) Award, 1952,* dated April 21, 1952. That award arose out of a dispute (Complaint No. 524 of 1951) reflected in a "log of claims" which had been submitted in 1951 by the applicant, the Australian Meat Industry Employees Union, to the Meat and Allied Trades Federation and others. The log of claims, presumably, amounted to a demand for an award to supersede "all previous awards made in this section of the industry." At any rate the proceedings before Conciliation Commissioner F. D. Kelly (held in Melbourne and Sydney at various dates in 1951 and 1952) culminated in the above-mentioned award—a seem-

---

[17] These rights and duties being specifically included among the "industrial matters" covered by the statute. New South Wales Coal Industry Act, 1946–1951, §§ 4(1)(k); 40(1)(d); 44(1)(a).
[18] *Dobb* case, 12 *IIB* 1142, at 1146.
[19] *Dobb* case, 12 *IIB* at 1150, 1151.

ingly typical code, containing 39 clauses,[20] and covering much the same
subject-matter territory that is covered by an American collective-
bargaining agreement. The dispute (or budget of 39 disputes) giving
rise to this award evidently was one over conflicting interests. Clause
34 of the award provides for a board of reference for each state. At
some time after the effective date of the award the Redbank Meat
Works Pty., Ltd., South Brisbane, presumably a member of the Federation and bound by the award, dismissed one Farthing (presumably
a member of the union and also so bound). The union protested the
dismissal. Also, (although the available record does not disclose it) the
union doubtless filed a complaint with the employer and requested
reinstatement of the employee. The union's complaint may well have
rested upon clause 6(b) of the award which, *inter alia,* postulated the
"right of an employer to dismiss an employee without notice for . . .
misconduct . . . ," the union asserting, presumably, that there was no
"misconduct." In any case, months after the budget of interest disputes had been resolved by the first award another dispute—a controversy of a very different sort—was precipitated by the dismissal of the
employee. The company having refused reinstatement, the union, turning to clause 34 (of the award) providing for boards of reference given
the responsibility, *inter alia,* "to settle disputes under this award . . .,"
on August 1, 1958, submitted its case to the (Commonwealth) Meat Industry (Shops and Small Goods Factories) Board of Reference, Queensland. No record of the Board's proceedings in the case has been available to this writer. However, it appears from the appeal record that
the Board "decided . . . that the lad misconducted himself" and that the
employer "acted within its right in dismissing him."[21] The union,
thereupon, pursuant to clause 34(f) of the award appealed to the Commonwealth Conciliation and Arbitration Commission.

The appeal proceedings duly came on in Brisbane on August 26,
1958 (and continued in Sydney in mid-September) before Conciliation
Commissioner F. D. Kelly, who had made the meat industry award in
the first place. Two representatives appeared for the union and one
for the company. One or more witnesses were called and gave testimony. The commissioner concluded that the Board decided correctly
and that it had "no alternative but to issue a certificate justifying the
dismissal. . . ."

---

[20] Set out in 73 *Commonwealth Arbitration Reports* 789–819 (No. A 2648).
[21] Australian Meat Industry Employees Union and Redbank Meat Works (Complaint No. 119 of 1958). Application to review the decision of the Board of Reference,
90 *CAR* 581. It appears from clause 34(g) that there probably were written transcripts
of the proceedings before the Board as well as written copies of its decision. These
items have not been available to this writer.

The developments in the *Farthing* case thus involved two industrial disputes: first, a many-layered controversy over conflicting interests (fully resolved, evidently, in the consent award); second, a derivative controversy, over conflicting rights under one of the 39 clauses, crystallized in a board-of-reference decision and an appeal from it to the Commonwealth Conciliation and Arbitration Commission. It is believed that these two disputes are typical of hundreds more: interest disputes over many issues—with batches of such issues resolved and bundled up into awards; rights disputes emerging severally out of one or another of the award clauses. This pattern probably accounts for a substantial proportion of all Australian industrial disputes, but there are many not thus accounted for. Some disputes on interests are settled, as at Broken Hill, by collective bargaining, American style; some, throughout Australia, are settled by prearbitral collective bargaining, sometimes by the parties on their own, but seemingly more often by the parties with the federal conciliator or commissioner standing by as guide, counsellor and friend;[22] some are settled by postarbitral collective bargaining negotiations for over-award rates. Rights disputes get settled by award variation, by board of reference, by court interpretations. In rare cases rights disputes find settlement through grievance provisions of awards or bargained agreements. Finally, all kinds of disputes, whether on rights or on interests, may get settled in Australia, as here, by the arbitrament of direct action.

Not only the nature of industrial disputes but also the techniques for dealing with them have been the subject of prolonged discussion in Australia. In 1918 the High Court, instead of taking the position that an industrial dispute was a controversy over what the parties to it could validly claim on the basis of existing rights, suggested that "[a]n industrial dispute is a claim by one of the disputants that existing relations should be altered, and by the other that the claim should not be conceded. It is therefore a claim for new rights, and the duty of the arbitrator is to determine whether the new right ought to be conceded, . . . [whereas] a court of law has no power to give effect to any but rights recognized by law."[23]

Reference has been made to the Commonwealth Parliament's pam-

[22] The president of the Commonwealth Arbitration Commission stresses the close kinship between conciliation and collective bargaining. He remarks that "conciliation . . . after all is bargaining." His Honour also says that "[a]s often as not . . . [the conciliator] puts the disputing parties into conference on their own," implying that often the prearbitral bargaining is not merely assisted bargaining. Sir Richard Kirby, "Some Comparisons Between Compulsory Arbitration and Collective Bargaining" 7 *The Journal of Industrial Relations* 1 (March, 1965), at 5, 14.
[23] Isaacs and Rich, JJ., in *Waterside Workers Federation of Australia v. J. W. Alexander, Ltd.* 25 *CLR* 434, at 463.

phlet dealing with conciliation and arbitration in which it commented
on the nature of Australian arbitration. That official report observes:

In the early years of constitutional interpretation, emphasis was laid on the
private-law analogy of commercial arbitration and on the essentially 'judicial'
character of arbitration. Since 1918 the emphasis has been . . . on the basis that
the Arbitration Court [now the Commission] is not limited to the adjudication
of existing rights and duties, but is authorized prospectively to impose a new
standard of rights and duties. The analogy is, therefore, that of a legislator[24]
rather than a judge, and the arbitral function has been held to be in aid of
legislative, not judicial power.

The pamphlet then refers to the observations of Isaacs and Rich, JJ.,
quoted above from the *Alexander* case, and continues:

The arbitral function is ancillary to the legislative function, and provides the
factum upon which the law operates to create the right or duty. The judicial
function involves first the ascertainment whether an alleged right or duty exists
in law, and then its enforcement.[25]

This judicial function has been exercised since 1957 by the Commonwealth Industrial Court. In that year the Conciliation and Arbitration
Court became the Commission. The latter tribunal had been in some
measure a court dealing with rights disputes, but was primarily a "legislature" dealing with those on interests. The Commission, formally
divested of judicial power, now devotes itself primarily to the business
of settling interstate industrial disputes on interest by the (quasi-legislative) process of conciliation and arbitration. The judicial functions
now are exercised by the Industrial Court. But there seems good reason
for thinking that the Commission, as a matter of practice, is not exclusively concerned with the legislative–arbitral function. Consider the
following very recent award provision: "The union concerned shall
have the right to bring a dispute concerning the suspension of an employee before a Commissioner or Board of Reference, or a dispute
concerning the dismissal of an employee before a Commissioner, for
determination."[26] Does not such an award provision for the handling
of a dispute about the suspension of an employee raise the question:
If the dispute about the suspension is brought before the Commission
(or even before a board of reference), is the determination something
arbitral or something judicial, that is, over rights?[27]

---

[24] The analogy, alternatively, might be that of groups of private bargainers negotiating, not a statute, but a collective bargaining agreement—U.S. style.

[25] Parliament of the Commonwealth, *op. cit.*, n. 7, p. 4 *supra*.

[26] *Slaughtering . . . Meat Industry Interim Award*, 100 *CAR* 305, at 314 (clause 7).

[27] Professor Mills notes that in the Commonwealth jurisdiction the settlement of
disputes on rights, in general, "involves exercise of judicial power which can be vested
only in courts." He points out, however, "that many cases of what are really rights
disputes are brought before the Arbitration Commission or before a board of reference . . . ," neither of which is a court. Mr. Mills concludes that in these cases the
tribunal "is more concerned with preventing a strike than with the nice technicalities
of constitutional law."

Chapter 5
Methods of Dealing with Rights Disputes

In Australia minor disputes are dealt with in a variety of ways,[1] of which the most important are the following:

1) By referral to specialized, tripartite boards of reference:
   (a) throughout the Commonwealth jurisdiction for "industrial disputes extending beyond the limits of any one state";
   (b) in Western Australia for intrastate disputes;
   (c) in coal mining in Queensland;
   (d) in the "non-arbitral" state of Victoria.
2) By referral to industrial magistrates.
3) By referral, for interpretation, to industrial courts: the Commonwealth Industrial Court, the Industrial Court of Queensland, or the Industrial Appeal Court of Western Australia.
4) By "award variation" by one or another of the major tribunals. Although this device is chiefly used for "legislating" amendments to awards in settlement of "interest" disputes, it may involve disputes on rights. The nature of the "variation" dispute may be difficult to determine.
5) By determinations by major tribunals. These determinations often are actually made by individual commissioners severally acting for a particular tribunal.
6) By direct industrial action.

Before scrutinizing more closely the half-dozen alternative procedures listed above for the settlement of rights disputes within the framework of the arbitral system—or, as with direct industrial action, operating squarely in the face of it—it is important to note that there is a missing link. The missing device is that of settlement in the shop where grievances, the most important of all rights disputes, erupt. Of course, a great many industrial grievances no doubt get settled somehow, offhand and informally, at their shop points of origin. But many, probably most, of them go by default. What seems lacking is the provision of

---

[1] This list is by no means exhaustive. Moreover, the methods are not mutually exclusive: for example, determination by a major tribunal may or may not involve resort to award variation.

more formal arrangements for grievance settlement in the shop. Strong evidence for the conslusion that most industrial grievances are given scant, if any, attention at the point of eruption is the extraordinarily heavy percentage of Australian strikes having a duration of one day or less.[2] There is good reason to believe that most of these brief "walk-offs" are caused by neglected and ignored shop grievances. But Professor Laffer comments: "The one-day strike is a sign not of poor grievance procedures but of the development of the practical use of the strike weapon for disputes over interests rather than the strategic use." Whatever the relationship between the one-day walk-offs and the frequency of grievance disputes, there seems to be no doubt that such disputes are very numerous.

At any rate, another well-informed Australian observer notes that ". . . by contrast to the position in North America, there is in . . . [Australia] no really developed system to deal with disputes arising out of the operation of awards."[3] This observation is buttressed by the findings reported after an intensive survey was made in the important iron and steel center of Newcastle, New South Wales. If one may judge from the practices there reported, it would appear that Australian employers pay relatively little attention to intraplant grievances. Among the steel companies in the region there is apparently little or no formal grievance machinery. This investigation points out that "great stress is laid on the role of the foreman." A "general absence of direct negotiation," even on major matters, was also noted. The steel companies generally "tend to discourage joint consultation." The investigator concludes that "[a]nything approaching collective bargaining or joint consultation is in most cases strongly opposed by company policies in the steel groups. In the non-steel group there is considerable willingness to seek solutions . . . outside the arbitration framework. . . . Wherever possible, management in the Newcastle area prefers to maintain a paternalistic rather than a consultative approach to rank-and-file employees. When this paternalism meets with a negative response from the rank and file, the most common reaction is to have recourse to the legal sanctions provided by the arbitration system."[4] It is in point, therefore, to give careful scrutiny to these sanctions.

---

[2] R. G. S. Rutherford, "Duration of Industrial Domestic Disputes in New South Wales, 1951–1956: A Preliminary Investigation," *The Journal of Industrial Relations,* III (October, 1961), p. 107. See *infra* p. 105 *et seq.* where the causal relationship between many strikes and the inadequate attention given to plant grievances is considered in more detail.

[3] Deryck C. Thomson (Law School, University of Sydney), in a book review article in *The Journal of Industrial Relations,* V (October, 1963), p. 168.

[4] B. Gordon (Newcastle University College, New South Wales), "Industrial Relations Procedures in an Australian Industrial Complex," *The Journal of Industrial Rela-*

SETTLEMENT THROUGH BOARDS OF REFERENCE

Boards of reference (by the terms of the governing statutes) are very often specifically authorized to be incorporated in awards. This is one of the most common and most important methods of dealing with minor disputes.[5] Such boards, as has been noted, are specifically authorized by the arbitral statutes of the Commonwealth and Western Australia.[6] There also are boards of reference authorized in the wages board state of Victoria.[7] Once boards are set up by the authority of award provisions, either party may "call a board" as occasion requires. In some instances, according to Mr. Justice Ashburner, a presidential member of the Commonwealth Conciliation and Arbitration Commission, reference boards are empowered to act of their own motion.

Apparently referring to boards of reference generally, Professor Kingsley Laffer observes that they "largely legislate about particular matters under delegated authority [conferred by the terms of the relevant awards]." He adds: "Though they may deal incidentally and probably illegally with rights disputes, this is not their prime function." The delegations of authority set out in the relevant awards vary widely. In some cases they are quite concise; in others they are extremely elaborate. Simple or elaborate, the odds seem to be that the authority delegated will include language like the following in clause 25(c)(i) of the *Coal Mining Industry (Electrical & Engineering Trades) Award, 1954 Queensland* (Print No. CR 1063): "The functions of the Board of Reference shall be—(i) the settlement of disputes arising out of any of the terms of this award; . . ."

---

tions, V (1963), pp. 160–165. The "Industrial Complex" dealt with by Mr. Gordon evidently refers primarily to The Broken Hill Pty., Ltd., which Professor Laffer considers "rather exceptional and extreme in its resistance to the development of informal relationships with unions."

[5] "Interpretation must be left to the judicial process. Decisions on actions, however, [such as e.g., discharges] can be handled more simply [by boards of reference]." F. T. de Vyver, "Australian Boards of Reference," 10 *Labor Law Journal* (May, 1959), p. 317.

[6] Commonwealth Conciliation and Arbitration Act, 1904–1964, § 50; Western Australia: (1) for industry generally, Industrial Arbitration Act, 1912–1963, § 89; (2) for coal mining, Mining Act, 1904–1957, §§ 321, 322. Although there appears to be no explicit statutory authorization, the *Coal Mining Industry (Miners) Award, 1954, Queensland,* made under the (Commonwealth) Coal Industry Act, 1946–1954, provides in cl. 21 for a board of reference for coal mining in Queensland. But the *Coal Mining Industry (Miners) Award, New South Wales* (made by authority of the same statute as the Queensland award just cited) contains no board-of-reference clause. It does, however, incorporate a "disputes" clause. The (Commonwealth) Coal Industry Act, as has been noted, is one of a pair of identical statutes, the other being the New South Wales Coal Industry Act, 1946–1951. Both make provisions for the Coal Industry Tribunal, local coal authorities and mine conciliation committees, all of which have something to do with settlement of grievances.

[7] Labour and Industry Act, § 31.

This "award language," or phraseology very like it, appears repeatedely in federal award clauses constituting boards of reference. It seems to authorize (and perhaps even to require) such boards to deal with all kinds of disputes, whether over rights or over interests. At any rate this writer finds it difficult to conclude that a tribunal empowered to settle "disputes arising out of any of the terms" of an award must be deemed not to have power to settle *all* disputes so arising.

But the resolution of the matter does not turn only upon award language. It also depends—and no less importantly—upon the words of the statute under which awards are authorized. That statute is the *Conciliation and Arbitration Act, 1904–1964,* which, *inter alia,* has created the Commonwealth Conciliation and Arbitration Commission, giving it jurisdiction to make awards and to appoint boards of reference. This power to set up such boards authorizes the Commission (in Section 50) to assign to each board so constituted "... the function of allowing, approving, fixing, determining or dealing with, in the manner and subject to the conditions specified in the award ..., a matter or thing which, under the award, may from time to time require to be allowed, approved, fixed, determined or dealt with by the Board." It has been suggested that the award language, quoted above by sample from a coal mining award, seems to authorize boards of reference to deal with rights disputes. But, for this writer at least, the implications of the statutory language of Section 50 are not so clear. This language seems to shed no light whatever on the question whether or not boards of reference are to be deemed authorized to deal with rights disputes. On the whole, in view of both the statutory and award phraseologies, there seems (to this writer) to be some basis for a contention that the boards should be deemed authorized to deal with rights disputes. But, apart from this writer's notions, the weight of informed Australian opinion appears to be that boards of reference may not deal with disputes over rights.[8]

Commonwealth Boards of Reference

By far the most important statutory authorization of boards of reference is that embodied in Section 50 of the Commonwealth Act. That

---

[8] "The fact that a Board of Reference cannot decide disputes over rights," says Professor Mills, "is of course a serious limitation, and one that is often ignored in practice, but I doubt whether the legislature ever intended the boards to decide such disputes." Professor Mills adds that "the phrasing of the legislation [under Section 50] suggests this." He remarks also that "there seems to be no reason why an award should not give to a board the power to vary the award ... [thus] it will still be dealing with interests disputes." Finally, Professor Mills observes that "if an award provided that the standard of misconduct which entitled the employer summarily to dismiss a man is to be determined by a board of reference in the event of ... any dispute about this, then such a dispute would be ... about interests, not about rights...." (Letter to this writer, dated July 26, 1965).

section authorizes the Conciliation and Arbitration Commission, by an award or by order, to appoint a board of reference and to assign to it "the function of allowing, approving, fixing, determining or dealing with . . . a matter or thing which, under the award may . . . require to be allowed, approved (etc.) . . . or dealt with by the Board."[9] Pursuant to this authorization the Commission has incorporated provisions for such boards in many awards and duly appointed them. The power given by Section 50 is almost invariably exercised by insertion of appropriate clauses in the awards.

It seems that most Commonwealth awards provide for boards of reference. The awards which make such provisions naturally prescribe their functions. The awards, following the somewhat tautological language of Seciton 50, authorize the boards to do what the awards authorize them to do! A more transparent way to characterize these prescriptions might be to say that the boards are authorized and instructed to settle industrial disputes "arising under" the particular awards. Whatever the details of the award prescriptions, they evidently may not be inconsistent with the terms of Section 50 of the Act quoted above. Those terms, in themselves, seem anything but constrictive, since the Act authorizes the Commission to appoint the boards of reference "for the purposes of the award." Awards being made in settlement of industrial disputes, it is to be expected that if and when such disputes arise in the course of their administration, those disputes also must be settled. Hence, boards of reference. Hence also, the awards' instructions to those boards, after more or less perfunctory reiteration of the statutory language, very commonly include reference to "the settlement of disputes on any matters arising out of this award."

Of course, it will not be a matter for surprise that these disputes "arising under" federal awards must be "industrial," must be "within ambit," and must be also, at least in theory, "interstate." This is not all. The settlements of the disputes "arising under" may not be judicial determinations. They must be arbitral settlements concerned with "the laying down of rules for future conduct," such settlements in other words as are within the power of the federal Commission in the initial making of the respective awards involved. The boards of reference no less than the Commission which creates them seem to be precluded from the exercise of any part of the judicial power of the Commonwealth. The statutory language of Section 50 of the Act is less explicit than, in some instances, are the award clauses which directly authorize the boards. Those clauses authorize, generally, the "settlement of disputes

---

[9] Section 50(1)(b) Conciliation and Arbitration Act, 1904–1964.

arising under" the awards. They sometimes explicitly bar the making of interpretations, but as noted below, the language often seems broad enough to permit them.

The following Commonwealth awards, *inter alia,* contain clauses authorizing the constitution of boards of reference. Some of the awards provide for many such boards:

The Metal Trades Award, 1952, as varied to October, 1960. (Print A 7470; original award published in 73 *CAR* 374) Clause 23.

Carpenters and Joiners Interim Award, 1952. (No. 589 of 1952; Print A 6053; 75 *CAR* 535) Clause 40.

Seaman's Award, 1955. (Print A 6961; 81 *CAR* 205) Clause 81, giving power "to the Industrial Registrar to appoint . . . a Board . . . of Reference. . . ."

Association of Professional Engineers, Australia, Award, 1961. (Print A 7856) Clause 9.

The Wineries Award, 1952. (No. 471 of 1951; Print A 7230; 74 *CAR* 869.)

The New South Wales Tramways and Omnibus (Traffic Section) Award, 1952. (Print A 2527; 73 *CAR* 703, at 727–740) Clause 31.

Slaughtering, Freezing and Processing Works (Meat Industry) Interim Award, 1962. (Print A 8600; 100 *CAR* 305, at 310–343) Clause 30—Board-of-reference provision; Clauses 6 and 7—termination provisions.

Federal Meat Industry Award, 1959. (93 *CAR* 659.)

The Coal Mining Industry (Engine Drivers' and Firemen's) Award, 1952. (Print CRB [Coal Reference Board?] 902.)

The Coal Mining Industry (Miners) Award, 1954 Queensland. (Print CR [Coal Reports?] 1057) Clause 21. [This award also incorporates, in clause 22, a paragraph entitled "Disputes."]

After brief comment on some of the awards listed above, and after considering the pair of Boning Room cases which arose under meat industry awards, a board-of-reference case stemming from the last award in the list is dealt with as the focus of a special episode: "the Case of the Queensland Coal Miner," which *sub nom, The Queen v. Gallagher,* finally came before the High Court of Australia[10] after exposure in 1962 to a federal coal mining board of reference and to the Coal Industry Tribunal. Since the successive decisions of board, Tribunal and High Court in this case come closely to grips with the significance of the dichotomy of disputes on rights and on interests, in the context of the constitutional limitations under which the Australian industrial tribunals function, the case of coal mine employee "R" will be made the subject of detailed treatment.

The *Metal Trades Award* empowers the several boards of reference established by it "to deal with," *inter alia,* "the settlement of disputes

---

[10] *The Queen v. Gallagher* [the Coal Industry Tribunal] and the *Australasian Coal and Shale Employees Federation* [the Union]; *ex parte Aberdare Collieries, Pty., Ltd.,* Judgment 24 July 1963 (18 *IIB* 633).

on any matters arising out of this award." The *Carpenters and Joiners Award* provides that "[i]f any dispute or question arises between the union or employees and an employer . . . work shall be carried on without interruption as a condition precedent to the exercise by the Board of any function in connection with such dispute . . . and the matter shall be submitted forthwith to the Board for its decision." The function of the board, it is further specified in rehearsal of the statutory language, "shall be to allow, approve . . . or deal with any matter . . . which . . . may require . . . to be . . . dealt with . . . and which, arising out of the terms of this award, may affect the amicable relations of the parties. . . ." The language of these two awards does not seem inconsistent with the idea that their respective boards of reference may make interpretations of award provisions.

The *Professional Engineers Award* sets up a board or boards of reference for the "industry of Professional Engineers" and assigns to them the narrow function of determining the qualifications of professional engineers. The Commonwealth Conciliation and Arbitration Commission, in its judgment in the Professional Engineers case, said in regard to boards of reference:

. . . the applicant [the Professional Engineers Association] suggested that provision should be made in the award for a Board or Boards of Reference pursuant to section 50 of the Act. The only objection . . . was the respondent's general objection that the definition . . . [of the terms 'Experienced Engineer' and 'Qualified Engineer'] posed problems that would be insoluble even by the Boards of Reference.

. . . we have decided to insert in . . . [the award] a provision giving the Commissioner . . . assigned to the industry of Professional Engineers . . . power to appoint . . . Boards of Reference . . . from time to time, consisting either of himself alone or of another person nominated by him, . . . [assigning to] such . . . Boards . . . the function of determining—

(a) Whether the adequate discharge of any portion of the duties of any particular employment requires qualification of the employee as (or at least equal to those of) a Graduate of the Institute of Engineers, Australia; and

(b) Whether any Professional Engineer who it is claimed is an 'Experienced Engineer' is . . . performing professional engineering duties . . . which . . . [require] qualification of the employee as (or at least equal to those of) an Associate Member of the Institution of Engineers, Australia.[11]

In the *Wineries Award* the board of reference is given the responsibility simply "to settle disputes as to matters under this award." In the New South Wales *Tramways Award*, the functions of the board of reference provided for by it include:

---

[11] Judgment in *Professional Engineers* case, 1961 (Serial No. A 7855), at 89. The award itself is Serial No. A 7856. 97 *CAR* 233–332, 344–354.

(i) The settlement of any dispute arising out of this award and/or any dispute between the parties within the ambits of the respective disputes concerned, but not involving interpretation thereof.

(ii) [The obligation] "to refer to the [Commonwealth Industrial] Court any dispute involving interpretation of this award.

The award further provides that "[a]ny dispute arising out of this award and any alleged breach of this award shall be referred to the Board of Reference."

Attention is now invited to fourteen industrial-dispute cases involving one or another of five important methods of dealing with rights disputes in Australia.

Preliminary examples of the settlement of grievance disputes under federal awards are two discharge cases—the "Boning Room cases"—both of which arose, under federal meat industry awards,[12] out of dismissals of boning room employees of Queensland meat-processing companies. The same union was involved in both cases, the Australian Meat Industry Employees Union. They are considered together at this point despite the fact that the Cairns Company case involved a federal commissioner and the Borthwick Company case a Commonwealth board of reference.

The Cairns Meat Export Company Case, the first of the two cases, came before the federal Commissioner (Gough) in 1962 on a union complaint against the discharge of four boning room employees in dispute with the Meat and Allied Trades Federation of Australia, and through it with the company. After hearings, and after the company's reinstatement of three of the employees, the Commissioner ordered reinstatement of the fourth.[13]

The company appealed to the High Court which sustained the appeal, prohibiting the commissioner's order.[14] The court's conclusion rested on considerations both of interstateness and of ambit. It considered that "[the commissioner's] . . . real authority was to settle any industrial dispute extending beyond any one state, but the matter was . . . not of that character . . . ," the High Court evidently considering the matter intrastate. Moreover, McTiernan, J., said: "I think that the reinstatement of an employee was not a subject within the ambit of the dispute."[15]

---

[12] They appear to have been substantially the same, or closely related awards: In the Cairns Company case, the *Federal Meat Industry Award,* 1959 (93 *CAR* 659); in the Borthwick Company case, the *Slaughtering, Freezing and Processing Works (Meat Industry) Interim Award,* 1962 (100 *CAR* 365).
[13] 17 *IIB* at 996 and 1113.
[14] *R. v. Gough and ors, ex parte Cairns Meat Export Co., Pty., Ltd.,* 17 *IIB* at 1212 (12 November 1962).
[15] High Court in *R. v. Gough, id.* at 1215.

The Borthwick Company Case occurred in 1964, two years after the happenings in the Cairns Company case. Here another Queensland meat-processing concern discharged a boning room employee. The union called a board of reference and its complaint duly came before the board, with Deputy Industrial Registrar N. M. Mansini presiding as its chairman. In this case the Meat and Allied Trades Federation appears not to have been involved, the union's complaint having been leveled directly against the company.

After hearings before the board the chairman said that "the evidence establishes beyond any doubt that . . . [the employee] was guilty of misconduct in leaving his work before the prescribed finishing time." After the conclusion of the proceedings "the Chairman recommended that, in view of . . . [the employee's] long and apparently satisfactory service . . . consideration should be given to his [conditional] reinstatement in the boning room. . . . Subsequently representatives of the parties met in conference and it was finally agreed to reinstate . . . [the employee]."[16]

There seems little question that if the board of reference in the Borthwick Company case had made a decision *ordering* reinstatement, the matter would have been appealed to the Commonwealth Commission, which presumably would have reversed the board. If not, the matter might well have gone to the High Court where there would certainly have been a reaffirmation of the Cairns case. The Cairns and Borthwick cases also furnish examples of the flexible way in which, given the same type of local dispute, a remedy may be had by resort either directly to a federal commissioner as in *Cairns*, or to a board of reference as in *Borthwick*. The availability of such alternatives as this is to the good. As the United States Supreme Court suggested in one of its decisions, "[w]e must remember that the machinery of government would not work if it were not allowed a little play in its joints."[17] This "play in its joints" of the Australian industrial arbitration apparatus no doubt results in its more effective functioning.

Boards of Reference in the Coal Industry

Preliminary Questions:[18] Boards of reference are not explicitly authorized by either of the twin coal industry statutes jointly enacted by the Commonwealth and the state of New South Wales.[19] Partly for this

---

[16] 19 *IIB* at 605, 606 (May, 1964).

[17] In *Bain Peanut Co. of Texas v. Pinson* (1930) 282 U.S. 499, 501.

[18] See also reference to Western Australian boards of reference in the coal mining industry, p. 83 *infra*.

[19] Coal Industry Act, 1946–1956 [Clth Print 2971/57] and Coal Industry Act, 1946–1951 [New South Wales]. The twin statutes directly provide for one-man or tripartite local coal authorities, appointed by the Coal Industry Tribunal. Commonwealth Coal Industry Act, 1946–1956, clause 37 (1) and bipartite mine conciliation committees, appointed by the (administrative) Joint Coal Board; *ibid.*, clause 42.

reason it seems desirable, before looking at the two coal mining cases which follow, to deal with some general questions raised by the arbitral arrangements for coal.

At least one award—the *Coal Mining Industry (Miners) Award, 1954, Queensland*—made under the Commonwealth "twin" by the Coal Industry Tribunal, incorporates elaborate provisions for a tripartite board of reference,[20] with an appointee of the Coal Industry Tribunal to serve as chairman. The functions of the board (set out in award clause 21) include "(i) the settlement of disputes arising out of any of the terms of this award," and (v) the settlement of all questions relating to contract or piece-work rates, with the qualification that "[n]othing in this award shall limit the right of any party to apply to the Coal Industry Tribunal for a variation of this award" (clause 21(i)). The Tribunal may review and alter the decisions of the board (clause 21(e)). Immediately following its board-of-reference provisions the same award includes, for good measure, the three-paragraph clause 22 entitled "Disputes" which provides, *inter alia,* that

[w]hen a dispute occurs at any colliery which cannot be settled by the manager, overman, and scrutineers, work shall proceed [as before] ... and the dispute shall immediately be referred to the appropriate industrial authority.

The last paragraph of clause 22 provides that

(c) In the event of any dispute arising as to the interpretation of this award or any dispute arising in the course of employment ... if such dispute be not amicably settled, it shall be referred to the appropriate industrial authority.

It may be presumed, perhaps, that the "appropriate industrial authority," twice referred to, is the board of reference. Yet that presumption may be wrong; the "authority" may be the Industrial Court. It may also be either the Coal Industry Tribunal which made the award in question, or the federal board of reference for Queensland provided for in clause 21 of that award. If the "appropriate industrial authority" is either of these tribunals, there arises (certainly as to the tribunal and probably also as to the board) a question of the assumption of judicial power by an arbitral body.

Not all awards made by the Coal Industry Tribunal provide for boards of reference. Thus, although its federal award for Queensland, as noted, contains such a provision, a parallel Commonwealth award for New South Wales[21] does not. Yet the latter award appears to have arisen about a month earlier out of the same dispute which gave rise to

[20] *CR* 1057. (Pamphlet, not published in *CAR.*)
[21] *Coal Mining Industry (Miners) Award, New South Wales, 1954.* Coal Industry Tribunal, Sydney, September 29, 1954. *CR* 1049. (Dispute No. 66 of 1952.)

the Queensland instrument. The New South Wales coal award does contain, however, a brief "Disputes" provision (cl. 26) which enacts that "any dispute arising as to . . . interpretation . . . shall be referred [in default of amicable settlement] to the appropriate arbitration authority."[22]

The circumstance (which seemed odd to this writer) that the Queensland coal award provides for a board of reference, while the parallel award for New South Wales does not, involves, according to Professor Mills, no such inconsistency as this writer had assumed. He comments as follows:

In the first place, the Coal Industry Act was concerned primarily with the coal industry in New South Wales: coal production was centered largely in that State (and still is) and the industry in that State had been most turbulent. The preoccupation of the Act with New South Wales is seen from the preamble to the Act and from the constitution by the Act of the Joint Coal Board to regulate many aspects of the industry in that State. In that State . . . there were also constituted Local Coal Authorities and Mine Conciliation Committees (§§ 37–43 [Clth Act; §§ 43–49, NSW Act]), and these were available to perform substantially the functions which elsewhere the Tribunal entrusted to the Board of Reference. [In the second place . . .] the Commonwealth and State Coal Industry Acts, as you say elsewhere, were "twins"; but they were not identical twins. The Tribunal, when wearing its Federal hat, has power to determine industrial disputes extending beyond the limits of any one State and for this purpose is given the powers of the Commonwealth Arbitration Commission under the Conciliation and Arbitration Act (which powers include that of establishing Boards of Reference) [§ 34], but, when wearing its State hat, it can deal with industrial matters confined to the State of New South Wales and for that purpose has the powers of the Industrial Commission of that State under the Industrial Arbitration Act. The State tribunals established under that Act have no express power to set up boards of reference and it has been held that an attempt to do so would be invalid: *delegatus non potest delegare;* furthermore, in the case of the Coal Industry Tribunal, an award setting up any such subsidiary arbitral authority would no doubt be held inconsistent with the express provisions in the State Act (and the Federal Act likewise) for the subsidiary Local Coal Authorities and Mine Conciliation Committees. Thus, although from one point of view it may be "odd" that there is provision in awards of the Tribunal for other States for Boards of Reference but none in New South Wales, there is ample explanation for this in the differing conditions and histories of the industry in the different States.

It has been suggested by Professor Mills that "it would be inconceivable that Gallagher, J., when making the [Queensland] award [in his official capacity as the Coal Industry Tribunal] intended to confer judicial functions on the Board [of Reference]" or, as the Tribunal, itself to exercise such functions. Professor Mills points out that "the vesting

---

[22] *Coal Mining Industry (Miners) Award, New South Wales, 1954.* CR 1049. (Not published in *CAR.*)

of the judicial power of the Commonwealth in *any* body would be the exclusive prerogative of Parliament. . . ." But whatever may have been His Honour's intent, the High Court of Australia evidently concluded that "The [Coal Industry] Tribunal unwittingly stepped beyond its jurisdiction," since "of course, it cannot make a judicial order."[23] The High Court found that the matters decided by the board of reference[24] and the Coal Industry Tribunal "were outside the jurisdiction of those two bodies" and involved "an attempted exercise of judicial power." The High Court "found that the matters decided by the Board of Reference and the [Coal] Tribunal were outside the jurisdictions of those two bodies. . . ."[25]

Depending upon the identity of the "appropriate arbitration authority" referred to in the "Disputes" clause of the Queensland coal award—or, possibly, irrespective of its identity—a question may arise as to the impermissible exercise of the judicial power of the Commonwealth, whether by a board of reference, by the Coal Industry Tribunal, or by any other tribunal. The High Court has shed light on that question as it arose in the circumstances of *The Queen v. Gallagher*. In that case, as noted, the High Court found that the questions decided by the Coal Tribunal and the Commonwealth Coal Mining Board of Reference for Queensland set up under clause 21 of the tribunal's award known as the Coal Mining Industry (Miners) Award, 1954, Queensland," . . . were outside the jurisdiction of those two bodies," insofar as they extended "beyond arbitral settlement by the laying down of rules for future conduct."[26] The High Court found that "the proceeding had been treated as one for an order for the payment of wages . . . [for] a past period, and as nothing else. [This was] . . . a decision which clause 21 of the award . . . could not constitutionally authorize, and there was no decision in arbitral settlement of a dispute arising out of any of the terms of the award."[27] The High Court found that there was a constitutionally impermissible assignment of judicial power to an arbitral agency. Since such disputes may involve issues of interpretation, application or enforcement as well as quasi-legislative issues as to wage rates, etc., the question is important. As to whether the referral of disputes (under clause 22(c)) "as to the interpretation of . . . [the] award," to the "appro-

[23] *The Queen v. Gallagher and the Australasian Coal and Shale Employees Federation,* Judgment of High Court, 18 *IIB* 633, at 635 (1963).
[24] Constituted by the Coal Industry Tribunal under clause 21 of its award entitled *Coal Mining Industry (Miners) Award, Queensland, 1954* (not published in *CAR*).
[25] *The Queen v. Gallagher and the Australasian Coal and Shale Employees Federation,* 18 *IIB* 633, at 642 (1963).
[26] 18 *IIB* 633, at 637 (1963). The award is set out in Print *CR* 1057.
[27] *IIB* at 638.

priate industrial authority" also constitutes assignment of judicial power to an arbitral agency, one can only suggest that the answer must turn on which "industrial authority" is fixed upon as "appropriate."

The first of the pair of coal mining cases which follow—the case of the Queensland Coal Miner—involves the question whether the Coal Industry Tribunal or the Coal Mining Board of Reference for Queensland had invalidly exercised the power of judicial determination of existing rights. The case was dealt with by the Commonwealth Coal-Mining Board of Reference for Queensland, a board created by the Coal Industry Tribunal when it made the Coal Mining Industry (Miners) Award, 1954, Queensland. The decision of the board was appealed, first to the Coal Industry Tribunal, and finally to the High Court.

The Case of the Queensland Coal Miner involves the Coal Reference Board, the Coal Industry Tribunal, and the High Court. The High Court of Australia recently handed down a definitive ruling on the powers of the Coal Industry Tribunal and of boards of reference with respect to judicial and non-judicial matters.[28] The court had before it rulings made by the Coal Industry Tribunal and by a (federal) board of reference for Queensland, established by the Tribunal in clause 21 of *The Coal Mining Industry (Miners) Award, 1954, Queensland.*[29] The first of the five enumerated functions of this board was that of ". . . settlement of disputes arising out of any of the terms of this award." The union applied to the board of reference in Brisbane for the purpose of determining a dispute arising out of the shifting of an employee, "R," a union member, from work in one mine to work in another mine operated by the same company. The union having objected to the shifting, R continued to report at the mine where he first was employed, but where the company gave him no work and paid him no further wages. He simply was "stood down" (laid off), but not dismissed.

Before the board of reference, the union had represented that it sought payment of wages to R for "each and every day upon which he has been refused permission to work." The *ex parte* members of the board were evenly divided, and the decision had to be given by the chairman, who "considered that . . . [R's] contract of employment included a . . . condition that he would be available for employment at

<hr>

[28] *The Queen v. Gallagher and the Australasian Coal and Shale Employees Federation,* 18 *IIB* 633–642. The Board of Reference having deadlocked, the chairman made its decision. (Print CR 1517, at 4.) The decision of the Coal Industry Tribunal, dated September 19, 1962, is published in 17 *IIB* 1047 (September, 1962). Compare: *The Queen v. the Senior Commissioner* (Melbourne Tramways case) 17 *IIB* 407 (May 4, 1962); and *The Queen v. Gough* (Cairns Meat Export Co. case) 17 *IIB* 633.

[29] This award evidently is not published in the Commonwealth Arbitration Reports. It is Print CR 1057.

any one of the mines . . . ," and that the employer's shifting of R from
mine to mine "was legally correct and reasonable" and concluded: "I
therefore refuse his claim for payment for all days he was idle when
management would not allow him to work at . . ." his first workplace.[30]

The union thereupon applied to the Coal Industry Tribunal for a
review of the board's decision. The Tribunal, after considering the evidence, "reached the conclusion that the employer had no right to transfer
. . . [R] from mine to mine without the concurrence of the . . . [Union]."
The Tribunal thought "that the Chairman should have decided that
the employer's right to transfer the employee . . . was conditional upon
the concurrence of the . . . [Union]." The Tribunal then added: "The
order of the . . . Reference Board is set aside, and the claim for an award
payment for each day in respect of which . . . [R] . . . has presented himself for work is hereby allowed."[31]

When the matter duly was appealed by the employer to the High
Court, that ultimate tribunal "found that the matters decided by the
Board of Reference and the [Coal Industry] Tribunal were outside the
jurisdiction of those two bodies. . . ."[32] The High Court stressed "the fact
that the matter before the Board of Reference and the Tribunal was, in
truth, a claim for wages . . . due and payable. . . . It is plain [continued
the Court] that the Board of Reference had no jurisdiction to adjudi-
cate such a claim; also that the Coal Industry Tribunal had no such
jurisdiction. . . ."[33] The court was of the opinion that both the board
and the Tribunal had invalidly purported to exercise the "power of
judicial determination of existing rights."[34]

Then the High Court came to grips with the essence of the matter.
The court did not question the power of the Coal Industry Tribunal to
make the award or to incorporate in clause 21 of that award provision

---

[30] Decision of the chairman (Print *CR* 1517, at 4).

[31] Decision of the Coal Industry Tribunal, 17 *IIB* at 1047, 1048 (September 19, 1962).
Up to this point, His Honour Mr. Justice Gallagher (a deputy president of the federal
Conciliation and Arbitration Commission) who is the Coal Industry Tribunal, was
dealing with the more technical aspects of the case. His Honour concluded his judgment with the following suggestion: ". . . I would add that the case is one in which
a cordial discussion between the representatives of the employer and those of the
Union would be of distinct advantage as a means not only of ensuring proper industrial relations, but of providing for an arrangement enabling . . . [R] . . . to continue in
his employment, and the company to use his services at the collieries under its control; . . . and the parties are accordingly directed to confer. . . ."

[32] 18 *IIB* 633.

[33] *Id.*, 633 at 635. (per McTiernan, J.) The High Court further held that the local
controversy which was involved "did not . . . constitute a dispute extending . . . and
[that] it was not within the ambit of the [earlier] dispute which was the foundation of
the award." 18 *IIB* 633, at 641 (per Taylor, J.). *The Queen v. Gallagher*, (etc.). Judgment, 24 July, 1963.

[34] *Id.*, at 637 (per Kitto, J.).

for a board of reference, charged with the responsibility for, *inter alia,* "the settlement of disputes arising out of any of the terms of this award." "But," the court continued, "one thing at least is clear. The power does not extend to conferring upon a Board of Reference any part of the judicial power of the Commonwealth. . . . If there was ever any doubt about this, the doubt could not have survived the decision in the *Boilermaker's* case. Consequently 'the settlement of disputes' in clause 21 of the award cannot extend beyond arbitral settlement by the laying down of rules for future conduct. It cannot include the giving of decisions in the nature of adjudications upon disputes as to rights or obligations arising from the operation of the law upon past events or conduct."[35] The application made by the union to the board of reference ". . . was therefore competent only as an application for a decision as to whether for the future . . . a direction by the management to . . . [R] . . . to work at . . . [another mine, laid] . . . a duty upon him to work there. . . ."[36] "Unfortunately, but perhaps not surprisingly," continued the High Court, "the consequences of the distinction betwen a power of arbitral decision in respect of the future and a power of judicial determination of existing rights and obligations were not observed when the matter came before the Board of Reference."[37]

The High Court's decision left to the Tribunal its central (legislative) function of settling interest disputes by award-making, and to the board of reference its function of settling disputes arising under the award. This last function, however, was conceived by the High Court as foreclosing to the board any jurisdiction to settle disputes about existing rights. It might not do anything judicial. The phrase "settlement of disputes" is a slippery one. It raises the question whether it is possible to act upon the full implication of the award's mandate to "settle" disputes arising out of its terms without being obliged to make, now and again, a judicial determination of existing rights. Yet the High Court held that neither the Tribunal nor the board of reference might exercise judicial functions. This holding would seem to bar both the board of reference and its creator, the Coal Industry Tribunal, from dealing with rights disputes insofar as the resolution of such disputes might involve the exercise of judicial functions or the making of interpretations.

The word "interpretation" is also slippery. That may be the reason why many of the board-of-reference or disputes clauses seem to fight shy of its use, stipulating simply (as in the *Gold and Metalliferous Min-*

---

[35] *The Queen v. Gallagher,* 18 *IIB* 633, at 637 (per Kitto, J.).
[36] *Ibid.*
[37] *Ibid.*

ing Award) that the board's functions "... shall be to settle and determine disputes and questions arising under this award."[38] This language surely covers disputes, the resolution of which requires the making of interpretations. As Mr. Justice Moore points out, it is "... necessary to be quite clear what is meant by interpretation. If interpretation is limited to mean the finding by some judicial body of the legal rights and duties which arise from existing law [including award provisions] with a view to the enforcement of such rights or duties or ... authoritatively defining them, then I think Boards of Reference in this sense cannot interpret awards because they cannot exercise judicial power."[39] Yet, as already noted, the Supreme Court of New South Wales (in the case of Dobb, a Local Coal Authority) has said that one of the functions of these coal authorities is judicial in the strict sense.[40] And, as Mr. Justice Moore points out, the High Court, in a 1960 case involving one Lydon (another Local Coal Authority) held that such an authority "could properly ... form views and opinions as to the meaning of words in a document." In the Lydon case the local coal authority (in this instance a one-man tribunal) "was settling an industrial dispute arising from a claim based upon a certain interpretation and the High Court held that he could properly do so." The High Court held, *inter alia,* "that the dispute was an industrial matter even though based upon a contention as to what the Coal Industry Tribunal meant...."[41]

The Cornwall and Sunrise Mines Case involves the federal Coal Reference Board for Queensland. This writer was fortunate enough in August, 1960, to have had the privilege of sitting in on some of the proceedings of the Commonwealth Coal Reference Board for Queensland in an adjourned session of a dispute matter[42] which had come before it some months earlier. The case had come before the Board under the authority of board-of-reference clauses in certain awards made by the Coal Industry Tribunal. The issue presented was whether the miners employed in the Cornwall and Sunrise Mines at Ipswich, Queensland, and covered by one or another of the awards of the Coal Industry Tribunal, should be required to break down large coal lumps to round ones about nine inches cube size; and if so required, whether the miners

---

[38] Clause 43(e). (1960) 94 *CAR* 700, 708–723, at 722 (Print A 7612).

[39] Letter to this writer, dated May 14, 1963. His Honour here speaks of the "odd result" that follows if boards of reference may exercise such interpretative (judicial) power, while their superior authority, the Commonwealth Conciliation and Arbitration Commission, seemingly may not do so.

[40] *Dobb* case, see p. 60 *et seq., supra.*

[41] *The Queen v. Lydon, ex parte Cessnock Collieries Ltd.* (1960), 103 *CLR* 15.

[42] Dispute No. 14, 1960. The Board was created under authority of clause 21 of the *Coal Mining Industry (Miners) Award, Queensland, 1954. CR* 1057. (Not published in *CAR.*)

should be paid three pence per ton extra for the work of "making little ones out of big ones" as claimed by the Queensland Colliery Employees' Union.

It appeared from the testimony and argument that the disputes, which had begun on May 27, 1960, had kept the Cornwall Colliery idle for eleven weeks. Miners at both the Cornwall and Sunrise Mines had staged a week's stay-down strike in protest against a refusal by their common management to pay a special rate for breaking down lumps of coal underground. It was asserted, evidently without contradiction, that the miners performed this work as directed for a period of three months from February 10 without extra payment.[43]

Shortly before adjournment the chairman put a motion made by a union member of the Board, that "1) It is not necessary for the coal miners at Cornwall mine to break lumps of coal. . . . 2) If the Board should determine that it is necessary for the miners to break coal underground, that 3d per ton be paid to the contract miners at the Cornwall Colliery for all coal filled." Upon putting the motion to a vote there was a deadlocked vote betwen the *ex parte* members of the Board. The chairman thereupon announced that, the Board not being unanimous, he would be obliged to issue a decision.[44] He did so, saying: "I am of the opinion that it was a term of the contracts of employment at Cornwall Colliery that the contract miners would, if required, break large coal lumps [to] round about 9" without [extra] payment, pending installation of crushing plant. [The relevant award evidently was silent on the point.] Claim for a payment of 3d per ton is refused. The foregoing are the opinions of the chairman, and the members not being unanimous, they become the decision of the Board."[45]

According to press reports, it appeared that work at the two collieries was resumed within a day or two following the conclusion of the hearings.[46] But this, of course, did not necessarily imply satisfaction on the part of the union or its members with the Board's decision. The acting secretary of the Queensland Colliery Employees' Union was reported as saying that his [union] "executive" was dissatisfied with the Board's decision, and he was also reported as saying that this ". . . was only a further indication of . . . [the unionists'] opposition to arbitration." The union president was reported in the same news dispatch as remarking

---

[43] A union representative on the Board remarked: ". . . what we desire from this Board is just merely common justice, not common law." *Minutes of Meeting* [of Reference Board] *Held at Brisbane on Monday, 29 August 1960* (mimeo), p. 32.
[44] *Minutes*, p. 37.
[45] Memorandum, Coal Reference Board Queensland, August 29, 1960.
[46] Brisbane *Courier-Mail*, August 31, 1960.

that "the decision of the Coal Reference Board was 'a clear indication of the fallacy of arbitration.' "[47]

The functions of this Queensland Coal Mining Board of Reference, according to its chairman, are mainly "the settlement of disputes arising out of [but evidently not limited to] the terms of the award, inquiry and report on matters referred to it by the [Coal Industry] Tribunal and the settlement of all questions relating to contract or piece-work rates."[48] The Board cannot vary an award any more than an American arbitrator may normally either amend a contract or make a new one. That is the function of the Tribunal. The chairman, further, indicated that the Board was not authorized to interpret the meaning of any clause in the award. That, he pointed out, was up to the Commonwealth Industrial Court. He suggested, however, that the Board could "make an arbitral interpretation; that is, lay down rules for the future guidance of the parties."[49]

Two questions about this board-of-reference case obtrude: (1) was the dispute within ambit, and (2) was it interstate? There seems good reason for concluding that the dispute was within ambit, although, since it did not involve the simple matter of wage rates, there is some room for doubt. The "settlement of minutes"[50] at the time of the making of the original award, and the topical range of subject matter of the award itself both seem to warrant the conclusion that the dispute about breaking up coal was within ambit.[51]

The answer to the question of interstateness seems to be "no." There seems to be no doubt that both the Cornwall and Sunrise Collieries are located in Queensland. If that is true it is difficult to understand how the federal board of reference was able to find a basis for assuming jurisdiction in the matter.

Finally, it should be noted that the dispute in the Cornwall Colliery case, like many other labor disputes, does not seem to be readily classifiable. Though a "minor" difference, no doubt, and an "industrial griev-

---

[47] *Ibid.*

[48] The board-of-reference provision of the governing award (clause 21(c)) states that among the board's functions shall be "the settlement of all questions relating to contract or piece-work rates." The secretary of the tribunal advises this writer: "It has been accepted by the parties that the . . . provision [cl. 21(c)] was within ambit of the original dispute." (Letter from Mr. J. Hills, dated November 25, 1964.)

[49] Interview with Mr. J. A. Murray (chairman of the board of reference) on August 23, 1960, and typewritten "Murray Memorandum" of the same date.

[50] "Minutes" (Black's Law Dictionary): "A memorandum of what takes place in court made by the authority of the court." In the context of award-making their "settlement" is a recapitulation—usually in the presence of the parties—of the award provisions, determined by the court, with possible amendments incident to suggestions by the parties.

[51] See n. 48, *supra.*

ance," it may be argued that it is one over interests. Certainly it is not as clear-cut a difference over rights as is a dispute about whether certain workers were entitled to the overtime pay specified in the applicable award. But the Coal Reference Board evidently assumed that it had jurisdiction under the joint statute and, more particularly, under the relevant awards. If those instruments incorporated what seems to have been the "standard" board-of-reference clause for coal industry cases, the Board in the Cornwall situation was under award mandate by the Coal Industry Tribunal "to deal with all complaints by employers or employees of breaches of the award or disturbances of customs of the industry not specifically dealt with by the award."[52]

Concerning coal awards in New South Wales, it has been noted that there are no provisions in the New South Wales Industrial Arbitration Act for state boards of reference, although Commonwealth awards applicable to that state, of course, may contain them. Apparently the awards applying to New South Wales under the joint coal legislation contain no reference-board provisions. However, a New South Wales award made by the Coal Industry Tribunal[53] does include a "Disputes" clause (cl. 26):

Disputes. In the event of any dispute arising out of the interpretation of this award or any dispute arising in the course of employment, there shall not be any stoppage of work either by the employer or employee in consequence thereof, and if such dispute be not amicably settled it shall be referred to the appropriate arbitration authority.

It would seem that here there is more need for a "Disputes" clause than there is in the Queensland award discussed above, since that award also provides for a board of reference. This New South Wales award, however, fails to specify which authority is the "appropriate arbitration authority." Nor is this specified in the Queensland award.

Western Australian Boards of Reference

Western Australia, as noted, appears to be the only one of the four "arbitral" states in the Commonwealth making provision for boards of reference for industry at large. In Western Australia, the Industrial Arbitration Act, 1912–1913, provides, in Section 89, that "the [Western Australian Industrial] Commission ... may ... appoint ... a Board of Reference ... and assign to ... [it] the function of allowing, approving, fixing, determining or dealing with ..." any matters or things that "un-

[52] For example, subclause (d) of clause 20 of the *Collieries Staff Award, Queensland,* 1956, *CR* 1189. Another part of the same clause assigned to boards of reference "[t]he settlement of disputes arising out of any of the terms of this award."
[53] *The Coal Mining Industry (Miners) Award, New South Wales,* 1954, *CR* 1049.

der the award or agreement . . . may . . . require . . . to be allowed . . ."
(etc.) by such board.[54]

The boards of reference provided for in the Industrial Arbitration
Act of Western Australia "are intended to function while the award is
in force, smoothing out difficulties and ventilating grievances as they
arise."[55] "The Court's [now the Commission's] power to assign authority
to the Reference Boards is somewhat restricted and must be limited to
authority over matters . . . arising under or out of the Award or order."[56]
"And its function is still limited in this manner, although the Board is
now . . . appointed for the purposes of the award 'or the industrial agreements as the case may be.' "[57] In Western Australia a "Board of Reference," we are told by a member of the former Industrial Court, "can
have no power to overrule an award. . . . Circumstances often arise
which were not anticipated at the time of the making of the award,
and in the light of these new circumstances adjustments might be necessary. Such adjustments could be made by a Board of Reference, but the
Board would not be justified in making any determination conflicting
with the provision of an award. . . ."[58] The board "could not possibly
alter [or vary] the provisions of the award,"[59] any more than an American arbitrator could modify in any way the provisions of a contract.

In the industrial agreement for engine drivers in woolen mills,[60] a
board of reference is created and assigned the "functions of (a) adjusting
any matters of difference which may arise . . . except such as involve interpretation of the provisions of this Agreement . . . [and] (b) classing
and fixing wage rates and conditions of any occupation or calling not
specifically mentioned in this agreement;[61]. . ." The power of "classing
and fixing wage rates" gives the board of reference wide scope indeed for
a subsidiary agency. Insofar as the occupations referred to are concerned,
this board of reference seems to be clothed with the same power to de-

[54] (Western Australian) Industrial Arbitration Act, 1912–1963, § 89.
[55] See A.W.U. (Goldfields) v. Lancefield (1938), 18 *Western Australian Industrial Gazette* (hereafter cited as *WAIG*) 201—footnote on page 101 of 1955 text of statute. The revised law (Industrial Arbitration Act, 1912–1963) is not annotated. Therefore the citations in this and a few of the following notes refer to the Industrial Arbitration Act, 1912–1952, as reprinted with annotations to March 31, 1955.
[56] See Wiluna Gold Mines v. A.W.U. (1938), 18 *WAIG* 66. (Footnote in 1955 text of statute at 101.)
[57] See Wiluna Gold Mines v. A.W.U., n. 56, *supra.*
[58] See Davies, A.P. in *Metropolitan Superphosphate Workers v. Mt. Lyell* (1937), 17 *WAIG* 423. (Footnote in 1955 text of statute at 101.)
[59] See Dwyer, P. in *A.W.U. v. Lancefield* (1938), n. 55, *supra.*
[60] Engine Drivers (Woolen Mills) Award No. 13 of 1960 (16 February 1960 to 15 February 1963); Clause 19. 40 *WAIG* 239–245. Parties: Federated Engine Drivers and Firemen's Union of Workers of Western Australia and Western Australia Worsted and Woolen Mills, Ltd.
[61] 40 *WAIG* 239, at 244 (clause 19).

termine wages and conditions (i.e., deciding disputes over interests) that is exercised by the Western Australian Industrial Commission and by the major arbitral tribunals in all of the other Australian jurisdictions. However, it lacks the power of interpretation presumably possessed by the Industrial Appeal Court of its own state and surely possessed by the South Australian Industrial Court as well as the industrial courts of Queensland and the Commonwealth. Another example of the delegation of broad powers to boards of reference can be seen in the *Railway Employees Award 1960*.[62]

It is interesting to compare the authorized functions of this engine drivers' Board of Reference with those involved in the American process of grievance settlement. This Board's task of "adjusting any matters of difference" apparently encompasses not only the sort of activities carried on here bilaterally, intraplant, in the course of the prearbitral "grievance" steps in the adjustment of "matters of difference"; it includes also—and here the similarity in function runs closer—the kind of work that is done by our arbitrators. But there are notable differences: (a) American arbitrators may, but this Board of Reference may not, interpret the clauses of the code involved—contract or award as the case may be; (b) American arbitrators generally may not, but this Board of Reference may, engage in "classing and fixing wage rates and conditions. . . ."

Apparently, boards of reference in Western Australia have very wide powers and may deal with disputes over interests as well as over rights, with the very important exception that they may not interpret. Under the cited statutory authorization incorporated in the Western Australian arbitration statute it appears that boards of reference have been provided for in many, perhaps in most, of the Western Australian awards. The provisions in the award for *Caretakers-Watchmen (State Electricity Commission)* seem to be frequently followed: the board is tripartite. Its principal function is "adjusting any matters of difference which may arise between the parties . . . except such as involve interpretation of the provisions of the award. . . ." It is provided that "[a]n appeal shall lie to the Commission in Court session, which is authorized to interpret."[63]

In some Western Australian awards there are incorporated provisions for special boards of reference charged with handling disputes arising

---

[62] Award No. 3 of 1961. See Western Australian *Government Gazette* No. 10, February 3, 1961.

[63] Award No. 29 of 1959. Clause 17. 40 *WAIG* 68, at 70. The authorization of appeal is in Section 89(2) of the (Western Australian) Industrial Arbitration Act, 1912–1963. Section 90 of the Act provides that "[w]ith respect to every award . . . the Commission by order at any time, while the award is in force, may declare the true interpretation of the award. . . ." The phrase "any matters of difference" (used in the enabling clauses of the award) would appear to allow the board to deal with disputes over interests, such, e.g., as are concerned with wage rates.

out of the elaborate award provisions concerning long-service leave. An example is the *Wool Scouring and Fellmongery Award.*[64] It appears that all of the Western Australian boards of reference are (like the one set up under the Caretakers' Award cited) tripartite and subject to appeal of their decisions to the Industrial Commission in court session.[65]

Special provision is made in Western Australia for boards of reference in the coal mining industry,[66] although this writer has happened across no record of the operations of Western Australian coal mining boards of reference, or even of the creation of any such boards.

Despite the existence of a state system of boards of reference in Western Australia, grievance disputes are sometimes settled (as they are in the Commonwealth jurisdiction) by a major tribunal. Such a dispute, dealt with by the Western Australian Court of Arbitration (now replaced by the Industrial Commission and the Industrial Appeal Court), is referred to below.[67]

Victorian Boards of Reference

In one of the two "non-arbitral" states, Victoria, which regulates its intrastate industry through wages boards, there is statutory provision made, nevertheless, for boards of reference. The Labour and Industry Act, 1958, provides that "[a]ny Wages Board may by determination provide for the appointment of a [tripartite] Board of Reference, whose chairman shall be [the person who is] the chairman of the wages board for the industry involved."[68] The same section also provides that such boards "shall have power to determine disputes of facts [but not of law] concerning any provision of any determination of the Wages Board which constituted it, but subject to a right of appeal to the Industrial Appeal Court . . ." to which court determinations of the wages boards also are appealable.

NATURE AND FUNCTIONS OF BOARDS OF REFERENCE

One-man Boards of Reference

Not all boards of reference are tripartite. The [Commonwealth] *Waterside Workers Award,* 1960, incorporates elaborate provisions for one-man boards of reference to be set up at the different Australian ports. The persons designated are the local representatives or local officers in charge of the Australian Stevedoring Industry Authority, or,

---

[64] Award No. 32 of 1959. Clause 28. 40 *WAIG* 89, at 93–96.
[65] Section 89(2).
[66] The Mining Act, 1904–1957, Part XIII.
[67] The case of the sacking of an employee smoking in a prohibited area (*infra*, p. 100).
[68] Section 31 of the Act.

in the case of a few of the smaller ports, "the person selected by the Registrar to be a Board of Reference...."[69] The award assigns to each of these boards an unusually wide range of functions, partly relating, it would appear, to disputes on interests. Those most relevant in the present context are:

(i) To hear, determine or report on all matters referred to it by this award for hearing, ... [etc.]

(ii) To ... report to the [Commonwealth Arbitration] Commission on any suggestion by ... the Federation or any employer for variation of this award to meet the peculiar needs of a port.

(iii) To encourage and facilitate the making of agreements in different ports on matters not covered by this award.

(iv) To settle disputes on any matters (not involving interpretation of any term of this award) arising out of this award...."[70]

Boards of Reference Under Industrial Agreements

Although not a frequent occurrence, it appears that in the Commonwealth jurisdiction boards of reference may be provided for in agreements made into awards as well as in awards made in open court, and they may be set up even under the terms of an unregistered (or unfiled) agreement. An example is an agreement, negotiated in 1958, between a large Australian manufacturer and an Australian union.[71] This agreement does something that is done in very few awards, and probably in very few agreements. It sets out a two-step grievance procedure for use "[i]f any dispute arises in connection with any of the Company's operations...." It then provides that "[i]n the event of the parties being unable to settle any dispute in conference, the party complaining shall, and the other party may, forthwith ... take proper legal action to refer such dispute for settlement to a Board of Reference, or other proper authority constituted under the provisions of the Act.... In the event of [such

[69] *The Waterside Workers Award,* 1960. Print No. A 6973, clause 28 (94 *CAR* 67–106; judgment at 3–67). The arrangements provided in this award superseded those which had been in effect, apparently from 1953 to 1960, and which provided for tripartite boards. The present arrangements reverted to an earlier system which had been in effect prior to 1953.

[70] As to the implications of paragraph (iv) in the text above, Mr. Justice Moore raised the question whether this means that only strictly judicial interpretations are prohibited to the board, or whether it also "precludes the kind of thing which was done in Lydon's case?" (Letter of May 14, 1963.) The case referred to by his Honour, *The Queen v. Lydon* (1960), 103 *CLR* 15, is noted on p. 80 *supra.*

[71] "... a branch of an organization of employees registered ... under the provisions of the [Commonwealth] Conciliation and Arbitration Act, 1904–1958 ...," apparently under Section 31 of the Act. The writer is not at liberty to disclose the identity of the parties to this agreement. Under Part X of the Act, industrial agreements (apparently *not* having the same effect as awards made under Sec. 31) may be certified by registrars. It appears to be the agreements made under Part X which do not provide for boards of reference. Industrial agreements made under Section 31 evidently may incorporate provisions for such boards,

legal action] ... not being available to either party, the dispute may by
agreement be submitted for decision to the Deputy Industrial Registrar
... or a person nominated by him, or in the event of the ... Registrar
being ... unable to act ... a person mutually agreed upon by the parties
hereto, who shall sit as an independent arbitrator. The decision of such
independent arbitrator shall be accepted as binding on both
parties. ..."

Functions of Boards of Reference

An American economist, Professor Frank T. de Vyver of Duke University, who visited Australia a few years ago, has made an intensive study
of the boards of reference.[72] Professor de Vyver concludes that the boards
"made no spectacular policy decisions nor do they interpret awards." He
recognizes the difficulty of drawing the line between the permissible application of an award clause and the impermissible interpretation of it.
It appears that by no means all Australian awards specifically preclude
boards of reference from making award interpretations. (The Commonwealth statute itself contains no specific prohibitions upon the making
of interpretations by such boards.) Moreover the language used in most
of the awards which provide for boards is such as to make it at least arguable that intrepretation was intended to be permitted. For example,
the boards of reference authorized by the Federal Meat Industry Award
were empowered "(i) To settle disputes as to matters under this award,
(ii) To deal with any matter directed by this award to be dealt with by
the Board of Reference, [and] (iii) To deal with any dispute affecting the
amicable relations of the parties."[73] This award evidently contains no
other instructions for the boards of reference authorized by it. It might
therefore be argued, especially in view of the language of (iii) above,
that whatever boards were set up would have power to interpret award
provisions. Unquestionably, a dispute about interpretation of an award
provision could very well affect "... the amicable relations of the
parties." The Commonwealth Industrial Court is explicitly empowered
in Section 110 of the Act to interpret such provisions, but, as remarked
above, it is not clear that this power is exclusive. Although the above-
enumerated grants of authority would seem to place no restrictions upon
the boards, a board of reference would not assume power to change or
"vary" the terms of the award; that would amount to legislating. In the
terms we have been using it would mean assumption of authority to

[72] "Australian Boards of Reference," *Labor Law Journal*, May, 1959.
[73] *Meat Industry (Shops and Small Goods) Award*, 1952, cl. 34. (Dispute No. 524 of
1951) 73 *CAR* 789, at 792–819. This award authorized the constitution of a board of
reference in each state covered by it.

determine disputes over interests. While a board of reference might bring about, so to say by right oblique (so narrow at times is the line between legislation and construction), what in effect would be an award variation, by the process of interpretation, that would seem to be the border-line limit.

Narrowly construed, the powers of the boards of reference are indeed very limited: they may not interpret; they may not modify; they may not enforce; they may only "apply." Here, in a sense, the Australian and the American concepts partly coincide. Both American arbitrators and Australian boards of reference recognize that they are dealing primarily with "minor" disputes on rights (arising during the terms of the award or contract). Seemingly, "major" disputes on interests are considered to be outside their purview. The American arbitrator takes on all kinds of minor differences, including not only those aptly described by Professor de Vyver as "action" disputes, but also disputes involving interpretation, even though, being justiciable matters, any of these minor disputes could be (and sometimes are) taken to the courts.

In America the arbitrator must not add to, subtract from, or "vary" the contract in any way. But he may interpret it—construe and apply its provisions—to any degree that he thinks proper. In Australia boards of reference may not "vary" awards in any way; to do that would be for them to "legislate" on interests. Nor, generally, may they interpret them, although as to this limitation there seem to be exceptions. The line of demarcation between the processes of legislative variation and interpretative variation, respectively, fades into invisibility and there seems to be a basis for the assumption (implied earlier in this essay) that award variation, though mainly a technique for resolution of "interest" disputes, may also fairly be—and is now and again—utilized for dealing with disputes on rights. For the American arbitrator to "vary" an agreement would be for him to abandon his ordained role and usurp the (private) legislative powers of the parties. He would be a party to the creation of "judge-made law." For an Australian board of reference to vary, perhaps even to interpret, an award would be for it to usurp the public, and "judicially legislative" powers of the major award-making tribunals.[74] It seems evident that boards of reference now and again, perhaps more or less unconsciously, make decisions which can

---

[74] Professor Laffer comments: "A federal award *cannot* give power to a Board of Reference to determine rights disputes as such, however much the language of the award may give a different impression. Boards of Reference, however, continually settle minor disputes over interests. The Commission, in effect, delegates some of its legislative power to them. For example, consistently with the award they may be required to determine rates for special classes of work or for work under particular conditions."

only be described as interpretative. It appears that awards sometimes specifically authorize the making of interpretations. Some Australian awards incorporate clauses headed "Disputes" which definitely do so, and these clauses surely are close cousins to "Board of Reference" clauses. The *Coal Mining Industry (Engine Drivers' and Firemen's) Award, 1952,* provides in clause 26: "In the event of any dispute arising as to the interpretation of this award . . . there shall not be any stoppage of work in consequence thereof and if such dispute be not amicably settled it shall be referred to the appropriate industrial authority."[75] One may guess that the "appropriate industrial authority" is the Commonwealth Industrial Court, as it just possibly might be the Coal Industry Tribunal.

SETTLEMENT BY REFERENCE TO INDUSTRIAL MAGISTRATES

Boards of reference have no monopoly on settlement of discharge cases. It is evident that such cases may be settled also by direct action, by an industrial magistrate, or by the Commonwealth Industrial Court. It is not entirely clear to this writer what considerations determine whether a given minor dispute gets settled by board of reference, by a magistrate, by the Industrial Court, or by strike. It may be entirely fortuitous, although the board-of-reference route clearly is closed if the parties to the dispute are not covered by any agreement, or if the award covering them makes no provision for such a board. In any event the conditions of settlement are essentially different in each case. If the resort is to direct action, the outcome is likely to be determined by the brute-power balance; if it is to the Industrial Court, there is a strictly judicial determination on the merits; if it is to a (tripartite) board of reference, the outcome may or may not be on the merits. Certainly there is likely to be a significant difference between the patterns of determination of a discharge case (or any industrial dispute, for that matter) by a bench of judges and by a tripartite (and, in major part, lay) tribunal.

In Queensland arrangements for settlement of local disputes (except, apparently, railway disputes) follow a formula in which the industrial magistrates play a central role. If the parties are unable to settle matters in conference "the nearest Industrial Magistrate" on application by

---

[75] Print CRB (Coal Reference Board?) 902. A "disputes" clause phrased in almost exactly the same language appears as clause 26 of the *Coal Mining Industry (Miners) Award, New South Wales,* 1954. (*CR* 1049) Still another "disputes" clause appears as clause 21 of the *Coal Mining Industry (Electrical and Engineering Trades) Award, Queensland,* 1954. (*CR* 1063) Clearly, the language of clause 26 cannot be said to clothe the boards of reference with power to make interpretations, except to the extent that the words "appropriate industrial authority" are *not* applied to the Commonwealth Industrial Court.

either party or of his own motion "shall convene a conference," make suggestions and endeavor to effect a settlement. "If no settlement is arrived at . . . the Industrial Magistrate may, and upon the request of any party, shall . . . hear and determine the dispute and his decision shall be binding upon parties . . ." subject to appeal to the Industrial Court. Thus, these minor disputes, as well as the major ones, may be settled by compulsory arbitration at the hands of the industrial magistrate, subject to appeal to the Industrial Court.

The Wool Presser's Case is an example of the settlement of a minor dispute by an industrial magistrate in the federal jurisdiction. This discharge case involves an employee of Grazcos Co-operative, Ltd. The employee, who was covered by the (Commonwealth) *Pastoral Industry Award, 1956*,[76] asserted before the Chief Industrial Magistrate that the company "had discharged him otherwise than for incompetence or misconduct. The complainant was employed by the Company as a wool presser . . . under a contract subject to the *Pastoral Industry Award*." The Magistrate, after listening to evidence as to the production record of the complainant on his job as a wool presser for the company, and "[a]fter indicating his agreement, by and large, with the submission put to him by . . . counsel for the defendant Company . . ." consulted the *Shorter Oxford English Dictionary* for the meaning of the word "incompetence." The reporter for the *Industrial Law Review* then quotes the Magistrate: "Adapting that [dictionary] meaning to the circumstances of this case, in my opinion the evidence establishes that Complainant was discharged for incompetence." The *Industrial Law Review* report concludes: "The Magistrate said he found that (a) the employee was discharged for incompetence, and (b) (if it was necessary so to find) that he was justifiably so dismissed."[77]

SETTLEMENT BY REFERENCE TO AN INDUSTRIAL COURT

An important method of dealing with Australian industrial disputes on rights is by reference to the Commonwealth Industrial Court (which has no legislative or arbitral functions) or, for intrastate disputes of this sort arising in Queensland or Western Australia, by reference to similar

---

[76] 86 *CAR* 645, at 667–702.

[77] *Australian Industrial Law Review*, Vol. 4, No. 22 (July 28–August 4, 1962). Case No. 173. In case of ". . . [b]reach or non-observance of any term" of any federal order or award, penalty "may be imposed by the [Commonwealth Industrial] Court or by any . . . Court of summary jurisdiction . . . or by an Industrial Magistrate. . . ." Conciliation and Arbitration Act, 1904–1964, § 119(1). Magistrates, especially industrial magistrates, also play important enforcement roles under the state arbitration laws. See, e.g., The Industrial Conciliation and Arbitration Act of 1961 (Queensland) Sections 97 and 116.

industrial courts in those two states.[78] The Commonwealth Industrial
Court is empowered to interpret and "to order compliance with"
awards.[79] These powers are part of the judicial power of the Commonwealth. Prior to the establishment of the court in 1956 these powers, as
well as the quasi-legislative arbitral powers, were exercised by the Commonwealth Court of Conciliation and Arbitration (now the Commonwealth Conciliation and Arbitration Commission). The Commission,
therefore, no longer exercises judicial power, its functions being primarily arbitral.

Many of the cases decided by the Industrial Court involve the interpretation of awards. It is "empowered . . . to give an interpretation of
an award." Applications for such interpretations, which are analogous
to the interpretations of labor contracts widely made by American arbitrators, are made "by an organization or person bound by the award."[80]
The Commonwealth Industrial Court has jurisdiction of all matters of
interpretation and enforcement where federal awards are involved, as
do the industrial courts of Queensland and Western Australia for intrastate matters of the same kind in those states. Three cases are presented to illustrate the handling of disputes by the Commonwealth
Industrial Court.

The Table Margarine Case is a recent example of a minor dispute
matter settled by interpretation by the Commonwealth Industrial
Court. It arose under the *Manufacturing Grocers Award, 1962*.[81] The
Nuttelex Food Products Pty., Ltd., a member of the respondent Victorian Chamber of Manufacturers, applied to the Commonwealth Industrial Court for an interpretation of subclause (e) of clause 9 of the
award. Subclause (e) did not mention the words "table margarine" but
rather noted that the employees engaged in the manufacture of table
margarine were covered by the award classification of "grocers' sun-
dries." The court unanimously held that these employees were not
covered by the award.[82] Conceivably, this particular dispute might have
been settled, alternatively, by application of the interested employer

[78] The Commonwealth Industrial Court, the Industrial Court of Queensland, and
the Industrial Appeal Court of Western Australia appear to be the only strictly
judicial tribunals in the industrial jurisdiction. For a comparative discussion of the
three tribunals, see D. W. Oxnam, "Recent Changes in the Western Australian Arbitration System," *The Journal of Industrial Relations*, VI (July, 1964) at 84.
[79] Conciliation and Arbitration Act, 1904–1964, §§ 109, 110. "The power to issue
mandatory orders for compliance with an award or injunctive orders against breach is
vested in [the Industrial Court] . . . alone." See Edward I. Sykes, *Strike Law in Australia* (Sydney: Law Book Co. of Australasia, 1960), p. 24.
[80] Conciliation and Arbitration Act, 1904–1964, § 110(2).
[81] Print 8321 (96 *CAR* 106).
[82] *Australian Industrial Law Review*, Vol. 4, No. 22 (1962), Case No. 160; 17 *IIB*
(May, 1962), 413; 17 *IIB* (July, 1962), 701.

party to the Commonwealth Arbitration Commission to have the award varied specifically to include table margarine.[83]

The Case of the "Dumpy Little Hausfrau" recently dealt with by the Commonwealth Industrial Court fits still more closely into the pattern of dispute situations commonly confronting our American arbitrators. It involved the discharge of a reporter employed by a Sydney newspaper under the discharge clause of an industrial agreement, which stated that "... the employer shall have the right to dismiss a member ... without notice ... for misconduct.[84] The matter was brought to the Commonwealth Industrial Court by summons (under Section 119 of the Act) in behalf of the discharged employee. The court had the case before it on September 10, 1963, on July 25, 1963, and on four days in April, 1964. Judgment was handed down on May 18, 1964. At the first hearing three judges sat; at the others, two.

The discharged reporter, who ran a "gossip column" in the Sydney *Daily Telegraph,* had included in his column, and attributed to a prominent Hollywood executive, a comment in "some overseas magazine to the effect that Elizabeth Taylor ... was 'a dumpy little hausfrau.' "[85]

The court held that the discharge was justified. Their Honours said:

In the present case the employee was guilty of a deliberate breach of his duty to report fairly, accurately and without improper distortion.... It was agreed that the position occupied by the reporter was one of more than ordinary responsibility. In these circumstances we are of opinion that his conduct constituted misconduct of such a degree as to entitle his employer to dismiss him without notice.[86]

The Overtime-Rate Case illustrates how diverse are the ways and means utilized for handling "minor" industrial disputes cases in Australia. This case "concerned the calculation of the overtime rate entitlement of an employee in the 'back of the house' at the Hotel Australia, Sydney...."[87] The employee's union asked the Commonwealth Industrial Court to interpret the pertinent clause of the (federal) *Liquor*

---

[83] Although the award provides for a board of reference (cl. 32), it delimits the board's power so drastically that it evidently would have been helpless to deal with the kind of situation described in the text.

[84] Journalists' (Australian Consolidated Press, Ltd.) Agreement, certified under Section 31, Conciliation and Arbitration Act, 1904–1959. The text of the Agreement is in 99 *CAR* 890–914.

[85] *Henry Gordon Coleman v. Australian Consolidated Press.* Judgment, 18 May 1964, 1. A condensed version of the judgment is published in 19 *IIB* (May, 1964), at 473.

[86] 19 *IIB* at 474.

[87] The case here summarized is reported in the *Australian Industrial Law Review,* Vol. 4, No. 23 (August 11, 1962), case number 181, and in 5 *Federal Law Reports* (June, August 1962) 89–94.

Trades (Hotels and Wine Saloons) Award, 1959, covering the employee.
The claimant union (Federated Liquor ... Employees' Union) appeared for the employee, the Australian Hotels Association for the
employer. The court was constituted by a two-judge bench. After hearing the parties, the court "held that on the true meaning and intent of
the award ... the claimant [Union] was right on its contention as to
[the method of calculation] ... and the award should be interpreted
accordingly."

SETTLEMENT BY AWARD VARIATION

The settlement of industrial disputes by award variation is a technique used mostly for the quasi-legislative adjustment of disputes on
interests. It is sometimes used, however, as a convenient expedient for
settlement of disputes over rights. Even in the case of those Commonwealth and Western Australian awards—and there are many such—
which provide for the constitution of boards of reference, and where
such boards have been set up, minor disputes are quite often settled by
the expedient of award variation by a major tribunal.[88]

The Dining Room Case, referred to the Commonwealth Conciliation
and Arbitration Commission, arose under the *Clothing Trades Award,
1960,* which stipulated that every employer of more than ten employees
must provide a dining room. A respondent employer in South Australia
refused to comply. An application for an order varying the award was
heard by a commissioner of the Commonwealth Conciliation and Arbitration Commission, who, being satisfied that the language of the award
was ambiguous, varied it "so as to ensure that [it] ... shall be applied
in the manner intended by the Commission." As varied, the award
provides that:

> (a) An employer of more than ten employees shall provide ... a dining room.
> (b) [Such an employer] ... may make application to the Board of Reference
> for exemptions ... and the Board ... may grant such exemption ... [if it]
> is satisfied ... that it is impracticable for such employer to provide the
> said dining room...," in which event the employer shall pay additionally
> to each employee, five per cent of his wages.[89]

It is important to emphasize that this use of the method of award
variation to settle a rights dispute is not its customary use, which is to
resolve disputes on interests. Award variation, for example, more likely

---

[88] Recourse to the expedient of award variation appears often to be had even in the
case of matters of interpretation which are among the chief responsibilities of the
newer vintage of industrial courts. See *Collier Trade (Marine Engineers) Award,* 1962,
clause 14. 18 *IIB* (March, 1963), 208. 99 *CAR* 188–198.

[89] Complaint No. 855 of 1962. Print A 8668.

than not involves simply an across-the-board increase (or decrease) in the hourly rates of wages of some or all of the employees covered by the award, or a change in hours of work or other conditions. It also may involve merely an increase in the rate of pay of a single employee. There is a baffling kind of ambiguity about this resort to the technique of "varying" an award, not only for the purpose of legislating changes in its terms, but also for the purpose of construing and applying it. It must be recognized also that what is said here about disputes on rights and on interests seriously oversimplifies the problem. The line between them is, at best, often a thin one. Sometimes it is invisible; one cannot determine in every instance whether a given dispute is one over interests or over rights. If only one employee is involved and he is the beneficiary of a change in the rate for the classification (in which he is the only person employed at the time), the dispute provoking the change might well be borderline.

SETTLEMENT BY REFERRAL TO MAJOR TRIBUNALS

Minor Disputes

As has been noted, even in the jurisdictions whose arbitral statutes provide for boards of reference for the handling of minor disputes, such disputes, nevertheless, are often dealt with directly by the principal tribunals.

It also has been pointed out that only in the Commonwealth and in one of the four "arbitral" state[90] jurisdictions, Western Australia, is statutory provision made for special procedures (utilizing boards of reference) for the handling of minor or grievance disputes. This means, of course, that in three of the four "arbitral" states the statutes have incorporated no provisions specially tailored for the handling of such controversies. In those states, therefore, minor disputes (except in the special case of coal mining) must be dealt with through the principal tribunals, whose central responsibility is the "legislative" determination of disputes over conflicting interests. The same tribunals, in other words, must handle not only "interest" disputes over what provisions shall be incorporated into the compendia of working rules ("awards"), but also "rights" disputes over the meaning and application of those provisions.

Nor are "rights" disputes over the meaning or application of award provisions (disputes "arising under") the only rights disputes that find

---

[90] Also, as already noted, the legislature of one of the two "wages board" states, Victoria, has provided for *ad hoc* boards of reference. Labour and Industry Act. 1958, § 31.

their way to one or another of the major tribunals. Such disputes can, and do, develop between employees and employers not parties to any award. Many local disputes come from time to time before one or another of the tribunals in circumstances which suggest that no awards cover the shops where the disputes have developed. Notable among grievance disputes without hint of awards are controversies about amenities and related factors, and disputes arising out of contested transfers and dismissals or other matters of tenure.

The arbitral laws of New South Wales and South Australia, as has been noted, do not incorporate provisions for boards of reference. The Industrial Court of South Australia and the Industrial Commission of New South Wales (which is "a superior court of record") both have extremely wide and varied powers, including the quasi-legislative award-making authority and the power of interpretation (stressed in Australia as a *judicial* power). It seems altogether likely, therefore, that much, if not all, of the kind of dispute-settlement business that goes to boards of reference in the Commonwealth, Western Australian, and Commonwealth–New South Wales coal mining jurisdictions must be handled mostly by the major tribunals in the other arbitral jurisdictions: viz., the Industrial Court in South Australia, either the Industrial Court, the Industrial Conciliation and Arbitration Commission or the industrial magistrates in Queensland, and the Industrial Commission in New South Wales (with some sharing of this load by the industrial magistrates in Queensland and by the conciliation committees in New South Wales). Finally, it must not be forgotten that much of the arbitral work is done by individual commissioners, especially in the important federal and New South Wales jurisdictions.

Although some Queensland awards give the parties an option at the outset whether to refer their disputes to an industrial magistrate or to the Industrial Court, the court appears to play a somewhat minor role in the settlement of local disputes. Even where the terms of the award give the parties an option, it appears that they prefer to go to the "nearest Industrial Magistrate." One reason may be that most likely he *is* nearer.

Grievance Settlements on Queensland Railways: Not surprisingly, a multitude of grievance controversies arise in Queensland out of operations under the *(1960) Railway Award—State.*[91] Its clause 85, "Interpretation of Award," provides that when a question arises as to award interpretation the "matter may be referred . . . to an officer [presumably

---

[91] The text of the award (dated November 18, 1960) appears in 46 *Queensland Industrial Gazette,* pp. 304–337.

a magistrate] designated by the Commissioner [of Railways]" and that if the commissioner considers his appointee's decision erroneous, the question shall be referred to the Industrial Court of Queensland for determination.[92] Under this or similar clauses in Railway awards a very large number of interpretations have been made. One of the simplest of them took the following form:

Question: (submitted by Amalgamated Engineering Union) A fitter employed at Mayne Running Shop is engaged on mechanical maintenance of diesel electric locomotives. Is he entitled to receive payment as provided for under clause 57(13) of 1952 Railway Award—State, in addition to his ordinary rate?

Interpretation: [by appointee of Commissioner of Railways] The shed at Mayne in which the diesel electric locomotives are attended is not a running shop. The fitter is not entitled to receive the allowance.

Decision: [on appeal to the court] The Court is of the opinion that the union's contention [that he is entitled to receive the allowance] is correct.[93]

The "interpretations" made under the Queensland Railway Award bear some resemblance to the awards made by the National Railroad Adjustment Board under our Railway Labor Act. Under that Act claims are filed with the Adjustment Board which, generally deadlocking on the cases, makes awards through neutral referees. There is an extraordinary parallelism, as to pattern and content, between these multitudinous local grievance cases on the Queensland railways and the analogous cases arising on our interstate railroads. Moreover, although there are important differences in the procedures there and here, both systems require compulsory arbitration.[94]

The following four cases have been selected to illustrate the expedient of resort to major tribunals for the determination of minor disputes. Two of them involve the Commonwealth Conciliation and Arbitration Commission, one the Industrial Commission of New South Wales, and one the former Court of Arbitration of Western Australia.

The Working Alleyway Case is an interesting example of a minor

---

[92] In 1960 the Industrial Court was the only state arbitral tribunal in Queensland. Its functions included both legislative award-making and judicial award-interpreting. In the following year, by the Industrial Conciliation and Arbitration Act of 1961, it was replaced by machinery on the Commonwealth pattern with an Industrial Conciliation and Arbitration Commission to make and amend awards and an industrial court to enforce and (ostensibly) interpret them. (Industrial Conciliation and Arbitration Act of 1961, assented to 11 April 1961.)

[93] 40 Queensland Industrial Gazette (March 31, 1955), p. 159. The fitter's dispute was submitted in 1955 under the terms of the 1952 Railway Award, whose clauses probably differed in some respects from those of the 1960 version, to which this writer does not have access.

[94] See National Railroad Adjustment Board (Chicago) Awards. (U. S. Railway Labor Act, 1926, 1934 (c. 347, 44 Stat. 577, as amended.) June 21, 1934, c. 691, 48 Stat. 1185, USC Tit. 45, §§ 151–163.

dispute coming for settlement before the Commonwealth Conciliation and Arbitration Commission. The grievance situation developed between the Australian Institute of Marine and Power Engineers (the union) and Burns Philp and Co., Ltd., as owner of the motor vessel *Malaita*.[95] The matter came before the late Mr. Justice Foster, a deputy president of the Commonwealth Commission. The complaint turned on the alleged inadequacy of the accommodations provided, in a "working alleyway," for three day-work engineer officers. It was asserted by the claimant Institute that the use of the alleyway by galley personnel disturbed the rest of the three engineers who occupied three rooms located alongside it. The dispute evidently did not arise "under" an award. At any rate no award is mentioned in the *CAR* report of the case.[96] His Honour, with counsel for the parties, made an inspection of the vessel. In his "judgment delivered" His Honour said: "In my view no alteration is called for, but I have suggested . . . two methods by which some mitigation of this trouble, if it is a trouble, can be achieved, namely, some sound-deadening covering on the alleyway floor and some instructions to the personnel using the alleyway that they should exercise normal restraint in their voices if they use . . . [it] when men are sleeping there. . . . I would say therefore that the solution of this problem is that any trouble be mitigated so far as reasonably practicable. I make no order as to other accommodations. . . ."[97]

The Case of the Builders' Labourers is a recent example of a minor dispute brought before a major tribunal, the New South Wales Industrial Commission. This case was precipitated by a controversy about

[95] Complaint No. 21 of 1960. 93 *CAR* 521. The matter presumably was an industrial dispute within the meaning of the (Comonwealth) Conciliation and Arbitration Act, its focus on board an Australian ship evidently giving it the requisite "interstateness."

[96] It appears that the Australian tribunals (at least the federal) fairly frequently, and without inter-party stipulation, take jurisdiction of disputes between parties not covered by awards. In America the arbitrator nearly always finds himself dealing with a dispute under a contract. Where there is no contract the parties file a written stipulation posing the questions to be decided.
That the locale of the dispute, in the *Malaita* case on board an Australian ship, has even wider implications is stressed by Professor Mills who points out that in the Commonwealth jurisdiction, although the "central core" of authority is the conciliation and arbitration power, the trade and commerce power (Australian Constitution Section 51(i)) also is relevant. This latter authority, he notes "is not unlike the U. S. interstate trade and commerce power." Professor Mills continues: "The Conciliation and Arbitration Act, . . . dealing in Sections 71–75 with the maritime industry, not only empowers the Commission to deal with . . . industrial disputes by means of conciliation and arbitration, but empowers it to . . . determine 'industrial matters' relating to trade and commerce with other countries or among the states whether there is any dispute or not. . . . Thus, in this industry the Commission is not restricted to disputes . . . nor is it restricted to the processes of conciliation and arbitration. It matters little that there is (or is not) an award for the matter in question; if there is an award the Commission can change it and if there is no award the Commission can make one. . . ."

[97] 93 *CAR* 521, at 522.

the reinstatement of four builders' labourers between G. K. N. Lysaght, Pty., Ltd., and the Australian Builders' Labourers Federation. The case appears to have turned on the alleged refusal of the employees to work overtime. Presumably the employer and the Federation were covered by an award, although the report of the case in the Australian *Industrial Law Review* does not indicate it, and it is not clear whether the requirement that overtime be worked was an award requirement or a working rule of the employer. The case evidently was initiated by "notifying details of the dispute to the Industrial Registrar. . . ." The matter came before the Industrial Commission constituted by a single judge (Sheehy, J.). At the conclusion of the proceedings His Honour said, as quoted in the *Review:* "Although I find that the men were at fault in not persevering sufficiently to get the job completed I consider that the circumstances were mitigating and on the facts of their case their dismissal was unjust so as to justify the intervention of this Commission by way of reinstatement."[98]

The Meal Money Case is another example of a federal case involving a minor dispute on rights. It centered on the "meal money" provision (in clause 18), incorporated by consent in the (Commonwealth) *Transport Workers (Oil Companies) Award, 1961.* This dispute came before, and was decided by, a single commissioner of the Commonwealth Conciliation and Arbitration Commission, "following the failure of earlier attempts [possibly at a 'compulsory conference'] to settle the matter by conciliation." The Transplant Workers Union and a number of respondent employers were involved, and the employers, at least, were represented by counsel. At the end of the proceedings "[t]he Commissioner said that although the intention of the parties at the time of their agreement was plain, there was in practice a divergence of opinion as to the meaning of the subclause. . . . For this reason he . . . decided to amend the provision. . . ." In other words, he "varied," or rewrote, the award in such fashion, presumably, as to reconcile the parties. Thus in the "overtime rate" case the (judicial) industrial court interpreted the award—without altering a word of its text—while in the "meal money" case the (legislative) Conciliation and Arbitration Commission interpreted "a divergence of opinion as to the meaning" by legislating a change in the award text.[99] Two queries may be posed: (1) Might not the industrial court appropriately have dealt with the "meal money" case handled by the Commission, and the Commission handled the

---

[98] The case is reported in the *Australian Industrial Law Review,* Vol. 4, No. 22, Case No. 169.

[99] The award is in 98 *CAR* 658–675. The case is reported in the *Australian Industrial Law Review,* Vol. 4, No. 22, Case No. 163.

"overtime entitlement" matter dealt with by the court? (2) Might not both cases have been handled by boards of reference?

Under both the old and the new arbitral legislation in Western Australia, compulsory conferences may be convened if agreement is not reached, and the matters may be referred to the award-making body: the Court of Arbitration under the old, the Industrial Commission under the new, dispensation.[100] Therefore the sort of grievance case now to be cited, although it arose and was dealt with under the old, evidently could have developed in substantially the same way under the new, legislation.

Sacking for Smoking in Prohibited Area was a case referred to the Court of Arbitration, Western Australia. On August 3, 1962, the record of the case indicates, an employee, Donovan, was "summarily dismissed for alleged smoking in a prohibited area . . .," by his employer, Construction John Brown, Ltd.,[101] who claimed that the discharge was justified. The Amalgamated Engineering Union, of which the employee presumably was a member, protested the discharge. A newspaper reported that the discharge "caused 400 men to stop work on a lubricating oil project at Kwinana [Western Australia] . . . and stopped work on the project for 1½ days. . . ."[102] Under Section 171 of the statute then in effect the Court of Arbitration was authorized in the event of a dispute to convene a compulsory conference of the parties, and in due course one was convened and the court's president, Mr. Justice Nevile, presided over it.

The conference discussions evidently having been fruitless, the president, as he was authorized to do by the statute then in effect, referred the dispute into court.[103] The dispute so referred became "No. 194 of 1962." The president of the court, in referring the dispute to the full court, said: "I . . . President of the Court of Arbitration do hereby inform the Court that at a Conference held pursuant to the said Act at which I presided, it appeared that the matters . . . in dispute . . . could not be settled . . . and no agreement was arrived at. . . . I do therefore . . . refer all the said matters to the said Court to be heard and determined . . . as an industrial dispute. . . ."[104]

---

[100] See Industrial Arbitration Act, 1912–1952, § 171(1)(7); Industrial Arbitration Act, 1912–1963, § 171(1)(6).

[101] The official record of the case appears in 42 *WAIG*, pp. 611–612. A newspaper account of the case was published in the *West Australian*, August 16, 1962, under the heading: "Kwinana Sacking Not Justified, Court Rules."

[102] *The West Australian*, August 16, 1962.

[103] Industrial Arbitration Act, 1912–1952, § 171. There is no indication whether either Donovan or his employer was bound by an award or industrial agreement.

[104] 42 *WAIG*, p. 611. The parties listed included the applicant, Construction John Brown, Ltd., and, as respondents, the Coastal District Committee, Amalgamated Engineering Union, Association of Workers, and some six other unions.

The record discloses nothing of the proceedings before the Court of Arbitration except the remarks of its president, under the heading "Decision:" *The President:* "For these reasons (we wouldn't make any award in this matter) I at least think Donovan should be given the benefit of the doubt. . . . I would recommend that the company take it that it has not been proved that Donovan was smoking and therefore that he be reinstated. . . . The whole thing seems to me [to] be an unfortunate lot of incidents . . . for which nobody has been proved to have been blameworthy."[105]

Major Disputes

Occasionally a rights dispute may be determined by a major tribunal even though the parties to the dispute are covered by an industrial award and the award provides for boards of reference. This is likely to happen when the dispute is a major one seriously affecting many workers and jeopardizing community welfare. For though most rights disputes are minor affairs, not all of them are.

An example of such a major controversy, albeit one over rights, is the Lima Crane case handled by a major arbitral tribunal, the Industrial Commission of New South Wales. Early in 1961 the dismissal of a union delegate, Jones, employed in the Newcastle Steel Works of the Broken Hill Pty. Co., Ltd., resulted in a serious strike and a great deal of publicity. The case developed between that company on the one side and the Amalgamated Engineering Union, Australian Section, and the Federated Ironworkers' Association on the other. It will be referred to herein as the *Lima Crane Case.*[106]

Apart from the strike there were three questions involved in the dispute: (1) a demarcation, i.e., a jurisdictional, question about which workers should operate a new Lima crane; (2) the question of the dismissal of a single employee named Jones; and (3) the dismissal of eleven delegates of the Amalgamated Engineering Union. Questions (2) and (3) arose, directly or indirectly, out of the first question about which workers should do "certain work in connection with the extension of the crane's jib." Perhaps the chief significance of the case arises from the dismissal of the union delegates. All three questions were matters of disputed rights: viz. rights to the work on the Lima crane, and the rights of a dozen employees to jobs.

[105] *Id.,* p. 612. Mr. Davies (member of the court representing employees): "Agrees." Mr. Christian (representing employers): ". . . I personally think that [the employee] . . . was smoking and that this dismissal should be confirmed." *Ibid.*
[106] In the state *Arbitration Reports* the case is designated: *In re* Dispute at Broken Hill Pty. Co., Ltd. Steel Works Newcastle: No. 1 (January 24, 1961). *Industrial Arbitration Reports* 1–6; No. 2 (March 8, 1961). *Ibid.,* 48–68. New South Wales Industrial Commission. Richards, Beattie and Kelleher, JJ.

The award under which the dispute arose was entitled *Steel Works Employees (Broken Hill Proprietary Company, Ltd.) Award*.[107] The company duly notified the industrial registrar of the strike. A compulsory conference was called and was presided over in Sydney by Kelleher, J., a member of the Industrial Commission. The judge, "having failed in his attempt to solve the matter by conciliation," issued an order directing "immediate resumption of work," to be followed by "discussions on the matters in dispute . . . between the company and the unions concerned," with any unsettled issues to be referred "to the Commission for determination." The order was not obeyed. The strike continued and the Commission was informed by counsel for the company that 1346 tradesmen (skilled craftsmen) were on strike and 2631 other employees "stood down" (laid off).[108] In this grave situation the matter was "removed to the Commission in Court Session" (a bench constituted of the president and at least two other members) before which the parties were summoned to a second compulsory conference. The company and some ten unions were summoned to appear. The full bench had no less than nine hearing sessions between January 23 and February 16, 1961. The compulsory conference on January 23 and 24 resulted in an interim return-to-work order, after compliance with which the parties were advised that further hearings would be listed.[109] The strikers returned to work. Hearings on the matters in dispute began on February 6 and proceeded almost continuously for about ten days.

At the compulsory conference before the three-man bench it was ordered, as an interim matter, that the disputed work on the Lima crane was to be done by the crane crew. It is not clear whether there was any further action on this question. Between the second compulsory conference and the resumption of hearings on February 6, the eleven delegates who had been dismissed were reinstated. As to the dismissal of the single employee, Jones, the Commission, after hearing testimony from him and others, continued: "No case has been made out for an order directing his reinstatement."[110]

---

[107] Text of the award appears in 135 *New South Wales Industrial Gazette* at 408. The official report of the Lima Crane case says: "The dispute originated in a demarcation [i.e., jurisdictional] issue relative to work on a new Lima crane but that issue was overshadowed . . . by two other issues arising therefrom, the first concerning the dismissal of S. B. Jones, a delegate of the Amalgamated Engineers' Union . . . and the second the subsequent dismissal of eleven delegates of that union." *Arbitration Reports* (NSW), (1961) at 1.

[108] *Industrial Arbitration Reports* (NSW), (1961) at 2.

[109] *Industrial Arbitration Reports* (1961) at 6.

[110] *Industrial Arbitration Reports* (1961) at 68. The Commission, obviously, considered that it had power to order reinstatement. That power seems not to be explicitly

The Lima Crane case is squarely comparable to the disputes determined by private arbitrators in this country. Even a dispute of this magnitude might well be heard and decided by a single American arbitrator, although it is of a character which might well warrant its handling by a three-man (perhaps tripartite) arbitral tribunal. This observer believes that the same case handled in the American way would have been decided exactly as it was in Sydney. The arbitrator would almost surely have refused to award reinstatement.[111]

As already stated, the demarcation dispute was made the subject at the outset of an interim order assigning the work to the crane crew. Possibly a final ruling followed, but if so this writer failed to note it. In any event, if one may judge from the Commission's two pronouncements in the case and from this writer's fairly continuous attendance of the hearings (though without benefit of a reading of the transcript of testimony), it would seem that there was not a very adequate testimonial foundation built up for the assessment of the pros and cons of the demarcation question. Certainly it was given only cursory treatment in the judgment of March 8th. That judgment (unless this observer has missed part of the record) did not review and evaluate the respective merits of possible alternative assignments to work on the crane's jib.

Another dispute in which the New South Wales Industrial Commission took jurisdiction had to do with efforts by members of the Motor Omnibus Employees Association, who were employed as bus operators by the Wollengong Bus Proprietors, under the *Motor Bus Drivers and Conductors (State) Award,* to prevent the issuance of bus tickets by machine. After a hearing, the Industrial Commission (Mr. Justice Sheehy) affirmed the "rights of bus proprietors . . . to administer their fare collection system by the issuing of tickets through machines. . . ." His Honour further [directed] . . . that the unions ensure that their

---

conferred by the Industrial Arbitration Act, but the "general powers" conferred by Section 30 A would seem to permit it. Professor Mills notes that the federal Conciliation and Arbitration Act "does not give any court authority to order reinstatement of a dismissed employee," except that Section 5 confers a power of reinstatement in "victimization" cases. Apparently one of the reasons for Jones' dismissal was related to his activities in "arranging the summoning during working hours of a stop-work meeting on the plant." *Ibid.* Another reason, apparently, was leaving his workplace without permission. *Industrial Arbitration Reports* (1961) at 3.

[111] Professor Mills suggests that if the order of reinstatement "is simply a declaration of the rights of the employee under the existing . . . award, then it will be a decision on rights, but if the reinstatement order creates a new right in the employee . . . then the order will be a decision on interests." He adds that "many cases of what are really rights disputes are brought before the Commonwealth Arbitration Commission or before a board of reference . . . especially . . . cases alleging wrongful dismissal."

members abide by the terms of the award and operate the . . . machines when so required by their employer."[112]

The "rights-dispute" cases that have been dealt with in the foregoing pages were settled after consideration of them severally by a variety of tribunals, among them: the High Court of Australia, the Supreme Court of New South Wales, the Commonwealth Conciliation and Arbitration Commission (constituted by one of its members), and for the same case on appeal, the same tribunal (constituted by two [presidential-member] judges and a lay member); the Commonwealth Industrial Court, constituted by a two-judge bench; the Court of Arbitration of Western Australia; the New South Wales Industrial Commission; and for the *Lima Crane* case, by the Commission's full bench.

Insofar as one can fathom the nature and incidents of these cases from the incomplete documentary record, it would seem that all of them were rights disputes (though some of them were, arguably, disputes on interests) and, therefore, in this country would have been brought before single American lay arbitrators. Some of the Australian cases, under our system, might well have been settled in the course of the bilateral grievance steps taken "intraplant" before reaching the terminal arbitration stage. Very possibly, there would be as many as fifteen arbitrators—one-man tribunals all—implicated in the five cases. In cases like the meat industry hiring matters (the "Boning Room" cases) we would have no appeal, nor would there be in any of the other cases; and we would, therefore, perhaps less adequately safeguard the rights of the parties than they were safeguarded in Australia. Such a chore as was involved for the Commonwealth Industrial Court in making its elaborate overtime calculation in behalf of the parties in the Hotel Australia case is run-of-the-mill stuff for our private arbitrators, though perhaps few of our arbitrators would do as competent a job as seems to have been done in that case by Dunphy and Eggleston, JJ.

As for the "Meal Money" case, disposed of by a single commissioner of the Commonwealth Conciliation and Arbitration Commission by the well-seasoned Australian device of varying the award, an American arbitrator confronted with the same situation doubtless would feel

---

[112] *Australian Industrial Law Review*, Vol. 4, No. 22 (1962), Case No. 170. *In re* dispute between Wollengong Bus Proprietors and Motor Omnibus Employees' Association. The award text is published in 143 (NSW) *Industrial Gazette*, 185. His Honour's Judgment is in 162 (NSW) *Arbitration Reports*, 148–152. The order of the Industrial Commission is in 146 (NSW) *Industrial Gazette*, 185.

shy at the idea of amending the contract as the commissioner amended the award, since here it is not deemed permissible for an arbitrator to modify the parties' contract. The upshot might be that he would "construe" the contract instrument to mean what the Australian commissioner amended the award instrument to mean, and there would be a distinction without any more than a semantic difference!

The dismissals of the four builders' laborers no doubt would be handled by any American arbitrator worth his salt in much the same fashion in which it was handled by Mr. Justice Sheehy of the New South Wales Industrial Commission. Such cases as the wool presser's discharge problem in the pastoral industry, handled by the (Commonwealth) Chief Industrial Magistrate, are run-of-the-mill cases for arbitrators in this country, and they are taken in stride.

All in all, it is doubtful whether American arbitrators would have done a more competent job than was done in these cases by the Australian tribunals. Perhaps they would have done less well. On one score, however, in this writer's judgment, there is little room for doubt: the cost, in time and in money, of getting these particular cases settled in the United States would be no more than a minor fraction of what the settlements must have cost in time and in money in Australia.[113]

SETTLEMENT BY INDUSTRIAL ACTION

Strikes and Lockouts in Australia

Despite a prevalent Australian pattern of restrictive, or even prohibitory, legislation—using the term in a wide sense that includes statutory provisions as well as award limitations—strikes and lockouts do occur in Australia.[114] In this country, to be sure, we have a heavier strike incidence than does Australia; but in view of our generally milder legislative policy on strike control, one would expect that the incidence of strikes and lockouts in Australia would be even less pronounced than it appears to be.

There is no question that in both Australia and the United States trade unions not infrequently fall back upon resort to strike or the threat of strike as a pressure strategy in all kinds of labor disputes. American unions may resort to strike action, or threat of it, in situa-

---

[113] Professor Laffer comments: "If, however, one considers Australian grievance procedures overall, giving no weight to the large amount of informal settlement, it seems almost certain that the cost of our grievance procedures, for most plants of comparable size, is far less than . . . in the U. S. A."

[114] Australian limitations upon direct action make no distinction between strike or lockout activities stemming from rights disputes and such activities arising out of disputes over interests. See J. E. Isaac, "Penal Provisions under Commonwealth Arbitration," *The Journal of Industrial Relations* (Sydney), 110 (October, 1963), 113.

tions in which they believe such action seems likely to improve their bargaining position.

In October, 1964, five Australian unions went on strike against General Motors–Holden in South Australia. It evidently lasted only a few days, but it naturally caused much uneasiness in Australia. In the national Parliament in Canberra the Minister of Labour, Mr. McMahon, commented on it. One Australian newspaper reported that the Minister ". . . told the House of Representatives that the General Motors–Holden strike was being controlled and manipulated by a '. . . notorious member of the Communist Party in Victoria'. . . ." The same newspaper dispatch quoted the Minister as saying:

A fundamental point is that if this industrial action is successful it could well be a blow to arbitration.

The unions apparently think that having obtained as much as they can through arbitration they will use force and direct action to obtain whatever more they can from those companies that are weak enough to give in. . . .

This Government does not take sides except on the side of law and order and of the system of conciliation and arbitration. . . .[115]

The Minister was headlined in the Sydney *Morning Herald* as seeing in the General Motors–Holden strike an apparent "move to destroy arbitration." The Canberra dispatch in the *Herald* quoted him as saying in reply to a question in Parliament by a Labour Member:

Arbitration is the law of the land and arbitration is open to the trade union movement, including the five unions involved in the dispute with G.M.–H.

If the unions believe they have a just claim and if they wish to put it before the Arbitration Commission, a log of claims can be filed and would be heard within a short time. The initiative lies with the unions.

If they refuse to use the remedy open to them, only two conclusions can emerge. The first is that they do not think they have just claims. The second, which is much more probable in this instance, is that the titular leader today of the Amalgamated Engineering Union in Australia is determined to destroy arbitration in this country, . . .[116]

Ever since the publication, half a century ago, of Henry Bournes Higgins' "New Province for Law and Order" there has existed in Australia a widespread conviction (except among trade unionists) that resort to direct action is incompatible with resort to the arbitral tribunals. The unions and their members generally, despite recognition by the Labour Party of the incompatibility of strike action with compulsory arbitration, take the position that, regardless of the existence of the compulsory arbitration system, when the chips are down they

[115] *The West Australian,* October 14, 1964.
[116] Sydney *Morning Herald,* October 21, 1964.

still have the right to strike. Perhaps the feeling of the fundamental incongruity between resort to direct action and resort to the arbitral tribunals is nowhere more deeply rooted than it is in the fraternity of conciliators and arbitrators. A fairly typical pronouncement is one made by Mr. S. F. Schnaars in 1962 when he was the conciliation commissioner in Western Australia. He said:

Australia is one of the foremost countries in the world in the rather venturesome and still experimental process of carrying the law into the sphere of industrial relations. From the inception of the [Western Australian Industrial Arbitration] Act all political parties have recognized that strike action is neither compatible nor reconcilable with the acceptance by the Australian people of a scheme of arbitration with legally binding awards. To this extent the Arbitration Act has always prescribed that strikes or lockouts shall be the subject of penalty provisions.[117]

The Commonwealth government has published statistics comparing Australian, New Zealand, United Kingdom, Canadian, and American strike experiences for each year from 1945 through 1957. The figures indicate for each of the thirteen years the average number of working days lost per wage and salary earner in civilian employment. The figures suggest "on their face," this official report says, "that Australia's recent record in the matter of industrial disputes [strikes and lockouts] is generally worse than in ... New Zealand, [and] better than the United States. . . ."[118] Examination of the figures in the table puts the United States in perhaps an even less favorable light. In every year of the thirteen-year period, except 1945, our strike-and-lockout incidence was higher than Australia's—and usually by a substantially wide margin.[119]

This foregoing observation on strikes and lockouts in Australia is intended merely to serve as a prelude to the following outline of the Australian statutory restrictions upon strikes and lockouts and the award arrangements also bearing restrictively upon them.

Unfortunately it seems impossible to segregate strike statistics, either here or in Australia, in such a way as separately to indicate which strikes were in attempted redress of grievances, turning on rights dis-

---

[117] Re claim for a "Preference to Unionists" clause in Award No. 1 of 1964 Metal Trades Award [WA]. Claim refused (9 November 1962) WAIG XXXII, 684; 17 IIB (November 1962) 1339–1343.
[118] Commonwealth of Australia, Department of Labour and National Service, Industrial Disputes in Australia (Canberra: Commonwealth Government Printer, 1958), Pamphlet, p. 11. The tabular presentation of the figures is on p. 25 (Table L). Despite its title it seems clear that this report does not deal with industrial disputes generally but only, or at least primarily, with disputes marked by strikes or lockout.
[119] Id., p. 25 (Table L).

putes, and which were incidental to disputes on interests. In Australia
the statutory limitations on direct action do not discriminate between
such action in disputes on rights and interests, respectively. There seems
good reason to believe that "quickie" strikes—lasting from a few hours
to a day or two—are more likely than not precipitated by grievance
disputes, and, therefore, that the most numerous strikes are those arising
from disputes on rights.

Some of these "quickies" or walk-offs, perhaps most of them, are
relatively unimportant except to those immediately affected. But some
of them are very serious. An example is the strike at the Garden Island
dockyard in early November, 1964. The newspapers reported it as
having been precipitated by the action of the Painters and Dockers
Union in requiring "a leading hand to resign his position." A news
dispatch stated that "[o]n November 5th, 290 painters and dockers
went on strike in protest over" the man's employment as the leading
hand of a gang. The men returned to work the next day, however,
to await the hearing of the dispute by the Commonwealth Conciliation and Arbitration Commission.[120] "This strike," the Commission was
reported to have been informed by a representative of the Minister for
the Navy, "is a threat to the biggest dockyard in Australia and the
most important in the Southern Hemisphere to our allies."[121]

From time to time it is recalled by a tribunal, by a union, or by an
employer, that, under the arbitration laws, an industrial dispute means
any industrial dispute, big or little; and where a little dispute pops up
it is grist for the mills of the state tribunals where its intrastateness
precludes federal action. But it seems that the destiny of a heavy proportion of these "little matters," perhaps of most of them, is to go by
default, because the unions and the employers are so preoccupied with
matters on higher levels.[122]

Certainly there seems to be a vacuum at the shop level. And that vacuum seems often to be filled—not very satisfactorily—by the "quickie"
strike. There seems to be no doubt that the short, one-day strike is
relatively far more prevalent in Australia than it is in the United
States. One investigator, looking at the strike record for New South

---

[120] *Daily Telegraph* (Sydney) November 12, 1964. Professor Laffer observes that a
"high proportion of short strikes is about over-award payments though this may not
always be the reason given."

[121] *Ibid.*

[122] Professor Kingsley Laffer of Sydney University writes: ". . . as to grievances at the
plant level I suppose 99 percent . . . are dealt with on the spot, without arbitration
tribunals ever hearing of them. . . ." "The Working of Australian Compulsory
Arbitration," in Roberts and Brissenden (eds.) *The Challenge of Industrial Relations*
(Honolulu: East-West Center Press, 1965), Chapter 5.

Wales, reaches the conclusion that "[f]or all industry, by far the majority of disputes [strikes?] last only one day."[123]

James W. Kuhn, an American student of labor relations who visited Australia nearly a decade ago, reached the same conclusions. He noted also that ". . . short strikes, those of one day and under, have become a major feature of the [Australian] labour scene. . . ."[124] He expresses the belief that "the short work stoppages—unofficial strikes, stop-work meetings and walk-offs indicate unattended worker grievances and unrelieved frictions between the workers and the management at shop and plant level. . . ."[125]

The same writer, after citing the widespread incorporation of grievance procedures in American labor contracts, remarks that "the bulk of American union business is made up of grievance handling and local bargaining. . . ."[126] He continues:

. . . what has been most harmful to the development of any regular, responsible procedure for handling workers' job problems [in Australia] has been the typical management stand . . . that questions of transfer, promotion, hiring, firing, lay-off discipline, work scheduling, work standards, and [the] introduction of new machines or processes are exclusively matters of management prerogative.
. . . Few of the [Australian] unions provide for any recognized, formal union activity at the place of employment,[127] except for the collection of dues. . . . The [Australian] unions do not appear . . . to consider the shop problems of workers as matters of much union concern. . . . [R]esponsible union organization at the job level is rare. . . . Union activity and attention is [sic] largely focussed upon high-level, industry-wide negotiations carried on through the arbitration courts.[128]

In another paper Mr. Kuhn says, ". . . The whole system of industrial relations in Australia is based upon a rudimentary foundation which gives little protection against misunderstanding, hostility and

---

[123] R. G. S. Rutherford, "The Duration of Industrial Domestic Disputes in New South Wales 1951–1956: A Preliminary Investigation," 3 *Journal of Industrial Relations* (Sydney) October, 1961, at 107. The context seems to indicate that Mr. Rutherford uses the word "dispute" as synonymous with "strike." "Domestic" seems to connote intracompany, perhaps intraplant.

[124] James W. Kuhn, "Strikes and Australia's Industrialization," 28 *Australian Quarterly* (Sept. 1956)56–68.

[125] *Id.*, at 60.

[126] *Id.*, at 66.

[127] Clause 24, "Shop Stewards," of the *Metal Trades Award, 1952,* provides that "they shall be allowed the necessary time during working hours to interview the employer . . . on matters affecting employees whom he represents." Print No. A 9020. For a discussion of the rights and duties of shop stewards see Costain Pty. and Bldg. Workers Union, Print A 9564 (Decision of Commissioner Mathews, April 3, 1964); and World Services v. Boilermakers Society (Decision of Commissioner Hood, November 10, 1961). (98 *CAR* 646; Print A 8251.)

[128] Kuhn, *op. cit.,* at 62, 63.

petty strife at the shop level.... Union officials show indifference toward their members' shop problems and . . . shop procedures are rudimentary or completely undeveloped. . . ."[129] As for the high frequency of the one-day stoppages, he concludes that "[t]he ultimate cause of the high rate of these strikes . . . is the arbitration system and the unions' political movement, both of which have weakened the vital, day-to-day local collective bargaining. . . ."[130]

The findings of the two commentators who have been quoted (one Australian, the other American) seem incontestable, at least in respect to their conclusions about the predominance of the one-day strike in Australia. They are confirmed by the Australian statistics contained in the recently published *Labour Report 1962 and 1963*. Its figures for 1963 (for "industrial disputes" involving stoppages of work) indicate that 151 of a total of 222 strike disputes in coal mining, 205 out of 312 disputes in stevedoring, and 689 out of 1250 disputes in all industries combined lasted one day or less. The figures shown for 1962 were not greatly different.[131] The latest data are for 1964. They show that in that year 166 out of a total of 223 strike disputes in coal mining, 229 out of 317 in stevedoring, and 755 out of 1334 in all industries combined lasted one day or less.[132]

The statistics in the *Labour Report* do not indicate the extent to which the one-day strikes are local, or intraplant, phenomena. No doubt there is a strong probability that the very short strikes will be found to be, mostly, local or intraplant episodes. At any rate, recent research makes it clear that these intraplant or "domestic" disputes have assumed considerable proportions, at least in New South Wales. An article by an Australian investigator, R. G. S. Rutherford, clearly discloses the wide prevalence of such disputes in that state.[133] Moreover, although they throw no light on the proportions of the domestic disputes to all industrial disputes, the findings do supply precise information as to the "duration" distribution of these domestic disputes. Thus it appears that, in New South Wales in the six-year period from

[129] James W. Kuhn, "Grievance Machinery and Strikes in Australia," 8 *Industrial and Labor Relations Review* (January, 1955), 175–176.

[130] *Id.*, at 173.

[131] *Labour Report 1962–1963*, pp. 185, 186. The figures here given for industrial disputes involving stoppage of work carry a note, "a" at the tabular heading "Workers Involved," which reads: "Refers only to disputes involving a stoppage of work of 10 man-days or more," and this is reinforced by a similar statement of limitation on page 178 of the same *Report:* "The statistics relate only to disputes involving stoppages of work of 10 man-days or more in the establishment where the stoppage occurred."

[132] Press Release, "Industrial Disputes, December Quarter, 1964" (Commonwealth Bureau of Census & Statistics), Table 6.

[133] Rutherford, *op. cit.* (n. 123 *supra*) at 105.

1951 to 1956, 3505 out of 4745 coal mining stoppages, 232 out of 320 waterfront stoppages, and 154 out of 554 stoppages in other private industries had durations of one day or less.

The industrial disputes data, both from the official *Labour Report* and the Rutherford inquiry, conspire to demonstrate the extremely high frequency of the "one-day" strike in Australia. It seems warrantable to hazard the guess that the preponderance of the one-day strike—which is largely intraplant or domestic—is not unrelated to Australian policies and methods with respect to industrial relations at the plant level.

Limitations on Industrial Action

In all five of the Australian arbitral jurisdictions there are statutory or award limitations upon direct or industrial action by strike or lockout:[134]

(1) The Commonwealth: Formerly set out in the Conciliation and Arbitration Act, the federal restrictions now appear—if they appear at all—only in the industrial awards. It seems generally true that new federal awards when originally promulgated do not include any restrictions upon direct action. If during the term of a new award there is no "industrial trouble" in the way of strikes or lockouts or threats thereof, there will be no variation of it in that respect. But if trouble comes, particularly overt and repeated trouble, either party may approach the Commission with an application to vary the award to prohibit resort to direct action, such prohibition to be effected by insertion of a "bans" clause in the award.

A recent example of resort to this expedient is one involving the *Railways Miscellaneous Grades Award, 1960.*[135] Following "industrial trouble" the Victorian Railways Commissioners (employers) applied to the federal Commission for an order varying the award by insertion of a new clause, reading in part:

Prohibition of Bans, Limitations or Restrictions

(a) No organization party to this award shall in any way, whether directly or indirectly, be a party to or concerned in any ban, limitation or restriction upon the performance of work in accordance with this award.
(b) An organization shall be deemed to commit a new and separate breach of sub-clause (a) hereof on each and every day on which it is directly or indirectly a party to . . . such ban, limitation or restriction.

---

[134] In America the raliroads and public utilities in ten or a dozen states represent the only important areas of private employment in which we have substantial limitations (by custom or by statute) upon direct action. Strikes by federal government employees are unlawful (Taft-Hartley Act, § 305).
[135] The text of the award is in 95 *CAR* 744.

After hearing before a commissioner the application was granted and the award varied.[136]

Strike (or lockout) action by workers bound by an award into which "bans clauses" have been incorporated may be the subject of proceedings by any party to the award—usually in the Commonwealth Industrial Court. In the General Motors–Holden strike of October, 1964, such proceedings were instituted in that court by the company against the five unions involved. The awards by which these unions and their members were bound presumably contained "bans clauses." At any rate, it appears that the court, on October 20, imposed fines aggregating seven thousand pounds (Australian) upon the five unions for violation of the bans-clause restrictions.[137]

There is widespread opposition to the "bans clauses" among Australian unions, opposition which is reflected in a recent proceeding in the Commonwealth Conciliation and Arbitration Commission. In this action eight unions were reported to have filed applications to have "bans clauses" deleted from the award (the important *Metal Trades Award*) by the terms of which they were bound. In the course of the hearings, presided over by Commissioner T. C. Winter, the general secretary of the Sheet Metal Workers Union, addressing the commissioner in support of the application, observed that one objection to the "bans clauses" was "that when strikes occurred some employers took immediate action in the Commonwealth Industrial Court to avoid using conciliation facilities of the Arbitration Commission."[138] He is reported to have added the comment that "fines and legal costs which resulted from employers' alleged excessive use of the clause were a 'crippling burden' on unions."[139]

(2) New South Wales: In New South Wales and in the other three "arbitral" states the limitations on direct action are spelled out in the arbitration laws. The New South Wales provisions are somewhat more

---

[136] The text of the variation [amendment] of the award is published as Print A 9612. Redress for any breach of this new "bans" clause, if one should occur, would be sought from the Commonwealth Industrial Court. That tribunal has authority under the statute "to order compliance with an award proved . . . to have been broken. . . ." (Act, Section 109). It has the power further to punish, "as a contempt of the Court," violation of its orders, and to punish such contempts by imposition of fines, which may run to maximums of £500 for an "organization" (usually a union), £200 for an employer, and "in any other case," £50. (Act, Sections 109, 111.)

[137] *The Daily Telegraph* (Sydney) October 21, 1964. Recent news dispatches from Canberra report that the Commonwealth government "will introduce legislation . . . to prevent the excessive use of the penalty provisions of the Conciliation and Arbitration Act" and to "compel unions and employers to 'cool off' for two weeks and negotiate on a dispute, when there is a threatened breach of an award."

[138] "Harm Seen in Strike Ban Clause," Sydney *Morning Herald,* October 16, 1964.

[139] *Ibid.* The language quoted is that of a newspaper reporter, not a union official.

involved than those of any of the other three states, and no attempt is made here to do more than to summarize. The limitations are set out in Part X, Sections 98, 99 and 99A of the Act:[140]

Sec. 98. If any person . . . does any act or thing in the nature of a lockout, or takes part in a lockout . . . unless the employees working in the industry . . . are taking part in an illegal strike, the Commission may order him to pay a penalty of one thousand pounds.

Sec. 99. The following strikes, and no others shall be illegal:

(a) Any strike by employees of the Crown, or of any Minister, trust, commission or board exercising executive or administrative functions in behalf of the . . . State. [specifying the agencies]

(b) Any strike [with one exception] by the employees in an industry . . . [wholly or partly] regulated by an award or agreement. *Provided,* that any union of employees may render no longer binding on its members any award which has been in operation at least 12 months, if a majority of its members so vote.

(3) Queensland: Strikes and lockouts are prohibited unless authorized by a majority vote.[141]

(4) South Australia: Section 99: "No person or association shall do any act or thing in the nature of a lockout, continue any lockout, or take part in any lockout." [Penalty not over £500.] Section 100: "No person or association shall do any act or thing in the nature of a strike, continue any strike, or take part in any strike." [Penalty not over £500.][142]

(5) Western Australia: "A person who takes part in a lockout or strike commits an offense against this Act."[143] [Penalty, employer or industrial union, £500.]

Probable Effect of Limitation on Direct Action

An informed Australian writer, Professor J. E. Isaac, has been quoted in these pages as pointing out that the Australian statutes and "bans" clauses in awards do not differentiate between what are herein called disputes on rights and those on interests.[144] Consequently, it is well-nigh impossible to measure the effectiveness of the Australian anti-strike limitations (whether legislative or incorporated in the "bans" clauses of awards) with respect to the strikes precipitated, respectively, by the two kinds of disputes. However, this writer's impression is that while Australian strike (and lockout) limitations have been highly effective in cutting down the frequency of strikes causally related to disputes

---

[140] Industrial Arbitration Act, 1940–1959.
[141] Industrial Conciliation and Arbitration Act of 1961, § 98(1).
[142] Industrial Code, 1920–1960. Part II, Div. VIII, §§ 99, 100.
[143] Industrial Arbitration Act, 1912–1963, § 132(1), Part IX.
[144] See n. 114 *supra.*

over interests (predominantly wage-rate controversies),[145] they have been much less effective so far as disputes on rights are concerned. One reason for this impression is the continuing heavy frequency of the short walk-offs of one day or less, which seem to represent the variety of direct action which is causally related, for the most part, to disputes over grievances.

---

[145] Professor Laffer comments: "In these days of bargaining about over-award payments you overstate greatly the success of the arbitration system in dealing with disputes over interests. Its loss of control over the latter is the most critical aspect of its working at the present time."

Chapter 6
Australian Grievance Settlement: U.S. Style

Although the normal pattern of practice for settlement of disputes over rights, and perhaps other minor disputes in the Commonwealth jurisdiction, is that of incorporation in awards of provisions for boards of reference and the handling of such differences before such boards, there are at least two instances of a pattern strikingly similar to the grievance settlement arrangements which are so widely characteristic a feature of American collective bargaining contracts. However, neither case is one of an award in the strict sense of prescription by a tribunal. One is a consent award, with a four-step grievance procedure incorporated: the *Engineering (Oil Companies) Award, 1958,* cited below, an award of the Commonwealth Conciliation and Arbitration Commission, in which the Commission "accepted," among the terms of settlement worked out by the parties (11 oil companies and 7 unions), the provisions of clause 25 dealing with the "Settlement of Disputes or Claims." This clause sets out a four-step procedure for the settlement of such disputes:

(a) The matter shall be submitted by the shop steward to the industrial officer or other appropriate officer of the employer concerned.

(b) If not settled the matter shall be formally submitted by the State Secretary or other appropriate official of the union concerned to the employer.

(c) If agreement has not been reached the matter shall then be discussed between the head office of the employer and the Federal body of the union concerned.

(d) If the matter is still not settled it shall be submitted to a member of the Commonwealth Conciliation and Arbitration Commission whose decision shall be final and shall be accepted by the parties.[1]

Here is grievance procedure settlement, much in the American style, although the arbitrator is a public official or tribunal and is not chosen by the parties. This particular award contains no provision for a board of reference and it may be that the parties decided upon this procedure as an alternative. This type of substitute for the standard board-of-reference clause does not appear to be widespread.

---

[1] The Amalgamated Engineering Union (Australian Section) and others v. Ampol Petroleum, Ltd. and others (Case No. 1014 of 1958). "Engineering (Oil Companies) [consent] Award, 1958." Serial No. A 6559. (91 *CAR* 212, at 215–234.)

The other case referred to above is a brief agreement, certified on July 20, 1959, by the Commonwealth Arbitration Commission (under Section 31 of the Act), between the Transport Workers Union of Australia and Roche Brothers Pty., Ltd., and another. The grievance procedure is a four-step one set out in clause 5.[2] There is no board-of-reference provision.

In some of the Australian jurisdictions, as noted, the boards of reference are specifically barred (by award provisions, but not by the statute) from handling matters involving interpretation. In New Zealand both in the statute[3] and in most awards the differences referable to disputes committees are those "not specifically dealt with" (or "matters not provided for") in the awards, without specific reference to interpretation. Moreover these boards and committees appear to be not intraplant, or even intracompany, but rather intraindustry tribunals, unlike their American counterparts. Evidently a large proportion of Australian (Commonwealth) awards provide for boards of reference. In the Commonwealth jurisdiction the Act, as noted, authorizes the Commission "by an award" to appoint a board of reference and assign to it (without mention of interpretation) "the function of allowing, approving, fixing, determining or dealing with . . . a matter . . . which . . . may . . . require to be allowed, approved . . . [or dealt with, etc.] by the Board."[4]

It is not surprising to find a disputes-procedure clause (similar to the one in the (Commonwealth) *Engineering (Oil Companies) Award* noted above in the jurisdiction of South Australia whose arbitral legislation contains no provision for boards of reference. The clause appears in an industrial agreement between the Electricity Trust of South Australia and the South Australian Branch of the Australian Builders Labourers Federation. It runs as follows:

5. Disputes Procedure Clause

Subject to the Conciliation and Arbitration Act, 1904–1961 (Commonwealth) any dispute or claim or demand (in this clause called "the dispute") which comes to the knowledge of an officer of the Union shall be dealt with in the following manner.

The dispute shall first be submitted by the Union through a local representative to the supervising officer of the E.T.S.A. (hereinafter called 'the employer') and if not settled, to the senior local officer of the company.

If not then settled, it shall be submitted by the Union through the State Secretary or other appropriate official of the Union concerned to the employer's Industrial Officer.

---

[2] 92 *CAR* 875.
[3] Industrial Conciliation and Arbitration Act, § 176(1).
[4] Conciliation and Arbitration Act, 1904–1964, § 50(1).

If not then settled it shall be submitted to the United Trades and Labour Council of South Australia for negotiation with the Trust.

If not then settled, it shall be submitted by the Union or the employer to the Commonwealth Conciliation and Arbitration Commission whose decision shall be final and shall be accepted by the parties.

While the above procedure is being followed, work shall continue normally. No party shall be prejudiced as to the final settlement by continuance of work in accordance with this subclause.[5]

It will be noted that this disputes-procedure clause contains language making it "[s]ubject to the Conciliation and Arbitration Act, 1904–1961 (Commonwealth) . . ." and providing further that the dispute (if not settled by the grievance procedure outlined in the preceding paragraphs) ". . . shall be submitted . . . to the *Commonwealth* Conciliation and Arbitration Commission whose decision shall be final and shall be accepted by the parties." This interesting, and at first blush confusing, importation of Australian federal power into *state* industrial agreements duly filed and registered "in pursuance of Part II of the Industrial Code, 1920–1958 [the South Australian Arbitration Act]" provides an example of the complications which can flow from the elaborate dualism of the state and Commonwealth systems of conciliative and arbitral statutes and tribunals.

The employer party is the Electricity Trust of South Australia, a quasi-governmental agency. The majority of its employees are members of unions having interstate jurisdiction. Those unions are parties to federal industrial agreements, or federal awards, as the case may be. Other intrastate unions or state branches of unions registered interstate evidently have only a few members employed by the Trust. These latter, minority, groups are covered by state awards, or (as in the two cases cited) state industrial agreements duly given the effect of awards by registration. The bulk of the Trust's employees are covered by the federal *Metal Trades Award*[6] to which the federally registered builders' laborers and miscellaneous workers unions are parties. Although it does not appear that the Electricity Trust of South Australia is a direct party to the Metal Trades Award, it seems likely that it is an indirect party through membership in the Metal Trades Employers Association, or one of the other parties respondent to that award.

---

[5] No. 36 of 1962, filed in office of the (state) Industrial Registrar, July 3, 1962. The text of the agreement appears in the *South Australian Government Gazette,* July 12, 1962, at 66. An apparently identical clause appears in the Agreement between the Electricity Trust and the Federated Miscellaneous Workers' Union (South Australian Branch) (1962, No. 32).

[6] 73 *CAR* 324, at 413–477. (Serial Nos. A 2459 and 2460.) In this important case the discussion preceding the text of the award—perhaps properly to be called the "judgment"—runs to 89 pages, the award itself to 64 pages.

The Metal Trades Award, although it contains no "disputes-proce-dure clause" *eo nomine,* does incorporate provisions for boards of ref-erence. The award provides (in clause 23b) that such a board "shall be constituted," *inter alia,* for South Australia, "other than Adelaide." Its board-of-reference provisions, therefore, appear to apply to at least some of the employees of the Electricity Trust. And, of course, these provisions are subject to the Commonwealth Act and the Commonwealth Concilia-tion and Arbitration Commission. The provisions set out in the "dis-putes procedure clauses" of the Electricity Trust agreement, mentioned above, technically apply only to small "fringe" groups of persons em-ployed by the Trust. In these circumstances it is understandable that it should wish to tie in the disputes clauses of the state agreements with the somewhat similar board-of-reference provisions of the *federal* award governing the bulk of its employees, to make the disputes clauses of the state agreement subject to federal as well as state law, and in the event of *impasse* to make the federal Commission the ultimate arbiter for minority as well as majority groups of employees.

As to its hourly rated employees, the industrial officer of the South Australian Electricity Trust says that settlement of intraplant disputes, if not resolved in early stages, go to boards of reference if the workers involved are covered by federal awards. If they are covered, instead, by state awards, disputes to which covered workers are parties through their respective organizations are settled, if possible, by a kind of un-written grievance-step procedure which makes no provision for third-party determination in the event of deadlock. If there is a deadlock the parties, or one of them, take the matter to the (state) Industrial Court, usually by way of a claim for an award variation.[7]

Award variation, of course, is a common method of affecting changes in work rules—in settlement of interim disputes on interests—where such changes are desired before the terms of an award have lapsed. It is an expedient comparable to American contract reopenings. What is more pertinent in the present context is that this same expedient of award variation is not infrequently resorted to in Australia in settle-ment of disputes on rights. This seems most likely to happen in juris-dictions where neither statutes nor awards contain board-of-reference provisions.

In the states of New South Wales and Queensland where boards of reference are not provided, the expedient of settling minor disputes on rights by award variation would appear to be a most necessary one,

---

[7] Interview with Mr. T. Kent, Industrial Officer, Electricity Trust of South Australia, Adelaide, November 15, 1960.

even though it involves a device primarily utilized in settlement of major controversies over interests. But it must not be forgotten that in both of these states other statutory provisions are available: New South Wales has its conciliation commissioners and committees, as well as the Industrial Commission; Queensland has its Industrial Court. Even in the jurisdictions featuring boards of reference, there seems, nevertheless, to be frequent resort to the device of award variation albeit it is in the settlement of grievance disputes.

In Queensland, according to an official of the Australian Workers Union, intraplant disputes often are settled by exchange of letters incorporating agreement by the parties to certain adjustments (in wages and other matters) without involvement with the Industrial Court or any government official. Evidently the disputes so disposed of may be either disputes on interests or on rights.[8] Another labor official at the Trades Hall in Brisbane expressed the opinion that something very similar to American in-plant grievance handling goes on constantly in Queensland. There are, he said "thousands of instances of it."[9]

LOCAL DISPUTES IN AUSTRALIA AND IN THE UNITED STATES

There is nothing in Australia comparable to our widespread systems of intraplant grievance settlement and terminal arbitration. The result is that, without question, a far larger proportion of all strikes in Australia than in the United States are short, "quickie" walk-offs precipitated by intraplant differences lacking ready means of peaceable adjustment, and that the majority of these unadjusted disputes are over rights. Most American strikes are longer stoppages largely related to interest disputes coincident with contract renewals, and only a small minority of them are precipitated by intraplant "rights" disputes.

There is no question that a great many intraplant disputes are settled Down Under without conciliative or arbitral intervention, but those not so settled are said never to be adjusted by private arbitration.[10] Evidently, in the larger establishments there are fairly well systematized procedures for the settlement of intraplant disputes, but as a rule these are largely informal and unwritten.

Neither is there any doubt that many intraplant disputes, both in Australia and in this country, fail to get adequate, or any, remedial attention. However, in view of the widespread American system of

---

[8] Interview with Mr. Edgar Williams, Australian Workers Union, in Brisbane, August 29, 1960.
[9] Interview with Mr. Alex Macdonald, Secretary, Trades and Labor Council (Australian Council of Trade Unions), Trades Hall, Brisbane, August 25, 1960.
[10] Interview with Mr. R. L. Braddock, Chief of Industrial Officers, Vacuum Oil Co. (Aust.) Perth, October 24, 1960.

grievance procedures directed specifically to the handling of these minor disputes, it seems safe to say that a much larger proportion of such matters probably go unattended to in Australia than in this country. One cannot scan the Australian arbitration reports and fail to be impressed by the vast number of cases which turn on intraplant matters, many of them involving no more than a handful of employees—indeed, often centered upon a single employee. In fact, one gets the impression that in Australia a solitary "John Doe"—or a pair of them—is not infrequently the hero or the villain for or against whom a quite staggering amount of judicial thought is brought into play. Similar phenomena are observable in the United States but seem less frequently to involve engagement of the big official battalions in the handling of "minor" matters.

A recent case before the Commonwealth Conciliation and Arbitration Commission furnishes an example of the handling by a major tribunal of a case which was a major matter only to the one person involved. *The Queerah Works (Falls) Case* arose out of an industrial dispute at the Queerah Works of the Cairns Meat Export Company Pty., Ltd., in Queensland.[11] It appears that the Australian Meat Industry Employees' Union had applied to the Commission (Commissioner Austin) "to make an order that, subject to employment being available the . . . [Company] should consider W. F. Falls for the employment. . . ."[12] The Commission, by Commissioner Austin, refused to make the requested order. The union appealed the decision to a full bench of the Commission (its president, Sir Richard Kirby, a deputy president, J. Moore, and a lay member, Commissioner Hood). The Commission "[a]fter hearing evidence (including evidence additional to that given before the [original] Commissioner) and submissions . . . said it was unable to form the opinion that the matter was of such importance that in the public interest an appeal should lie."[13]

The Commission concluded its decision in the case with the following comment:

We are of opinion, however, that the parties might be assisted in their future relationships if some code of procedure were adopted which could resolve disputes as to engagements and dismissals with expedition and certainty. . . . The appeal being held not to lie, the application is dismissed.

[11] This case resembles in some ways the two "Boning Room cases" dealt with *supra* at pages 72–73. Though this small case involves only the question of the employment of a single individual, the dispute perhaps ought to be classified as one on interests.

[12] *Australian Industrial Law Review,* Vol. 4, No. 25 (August 25–September 1, 1962). Case No. 193. The first phase of the case was reported in Vol. 4, No. 20 (July 7–14, 1962) as Case No. 141. The relevant award, the Federal Meat Industry Award 1959 (93 *CAR* 659, at 660–693, Serial No. A 7329) provides in clause 34 for boards of reference. There is no mention of "interpretation."

[13] *Australian Industrial Law Review,* Vol. 4, No. 25, Case No. 193.

It should be noted that jurisdiction was taken in this small, one-man case on the ground that the union and the company involved were parties to an interstate award in effect at the time the *Falls* case was heard.

Soon after the dispute which precipitated the *Falls* case, a similar controversy arose at the works of the same company. Another commissioner (Mr. Gough), sitting as the Arbitration Commission, after hearing both parties made an order that as the company had not been justified in dismissing four of its employees it should offer to reinstate them. This case also might have been appealed, as was the commissioner's decision in the *Falls* case, to a full bench of the Commission. Instead the company successfully challenged the Commission's reinstatement order in the High Court of Australia on the ground that it was not within the commissioner's jurisdiction to make such an order.[14] Mr. Justice Moore of the Commonwealth Commission comments as follows on the High Court's decision:

[Its] . . . reasoning was that this was not an interstate industrial dispute and therefore not a matter with which . . . the Commission could deal. The limitation on Federal power in the Australian Constitution to the settlement of interstate industrial disputes precluded the Commissioner from dealing with this intra-state dispute, and as it was not a matter which had been part of the original interstate . . . dispute, which properly enabled the Commission to make the original Federal award, it could not have been . . . [a part of] the award made in settlement of that original dispute. Indeed, it is suggested in the judgment of the . . . High Court that it might be difficult to create an interstate industrial dispute in such a way . . . [as to make it possible for] an award to be made to confer power on a Commissioner to deal with a minor matter of this kind.[15]

The type of dispute situation which underlies the proceedings just summarized is a fairly common one in industry on both sides of the equator: union man wants former employer to hire him, his union supports him; the employer refuses. The dispute clearly is a "minor" one, whether it is on "rights" or on "interests." How it is to be classified may well turn on whether or not one accepts the idea that the union man has a "right" to an available job. In the United States, in a situation of this sort, if the bilateral grievance steps set out in the contract have been taken to no avail, the employer and the union, pursuant to their contract, bring in their arbitrator; or if they happen not to have made a

---

[14] *The Queen v. Gough*, and ors. *ex parte* Cairns Meat Export Co., *IIB* 1212 (November, 1962).

[15] Letter to this writer, dated May 14, 1963. The present writer ventures to raise the question whether the dispute created by the four dismissals precluded the commissioner from intervening not only because it was intrastate, but also because it was not within ambit. The issue of ambit was raised in the *Tramways* case 17, *IIB* 211, 407 (March, May, 1962).

contract providing for one, they sign a submission to bring in their jointly chosen man *ad hoc*. He hears the parties, evidence is called, and argument heard. He determines the dispute and hands down an award with an opinion (in Australia, a "judgment" with "reasons"). The American arbitrator's conclusions, if he has before him cases substantially like the two Australian tenure-of-employment cases just outlined, might well be the same. If he concluded that the employer should hire or reinstate the men, he would make an appropriate award, directing that they be taken on if and when employment became available. If his conclusion was that the men should not be hired or reinstated, his award would be to that effect. Whatever his determination, it would be implemented by an award and probably supplemented by a rationalizing opinion, and perhaps by a summary of the case situation including a recapitulation of the positions of the parties. And there, normally, the matter would end, the award being final and unappealable.

Chapter 7
Conclusions

Two suggestions are ventured in conclusion: (1) Boards of reference might well be even more widely utilized than they are at present. The institution definitely seems to be spreading, South Australia having introduced it in a limited way in 1963, leaving only Queensland and New South Wales without any provisions for such boards. (2) Industrial grievances intraplant might be usefully dealt with by the more general inclusion in awards of provisions similar to the step-by-step arrangements incorporated in the Engineering (Oil Companies) Award, and one or two others, already referred to.

BOARDS OF REFERENCE

These tripartite tribunals (with commissioners or industrial registrars serving as chairmen) seem to be unique Australian devices for dealing, more or less judicially, with disputes "arising under" awards which legislatively lay down the rules to govern the relationships of the parties for future terms. As an auxiliary arbitral device for settlement of rights disputes, within a system chiefly devoted to the legislative arbitration of disputes on interests, the board of reference seems to have been an essential development.[1]

As rights disputes multiplied with the multiplication of awards, the major tribunals faced the necessity, in default of devices such as boards of reference, of dealing with small grievance matters as well as with the interest-dispute matters which continued to be their chief concern. As boards of reference and, later, non-arbitral industrial courts, have emerged in some jurisdictions, the major arbitral tribunals have there been freed of the necessity for dealing with rights disputes. Yet, for whatever reason, perhaps institutional force of habit, the major tribunals even in these jurisdictions continue to concern themselves with these minor matters. This is true today in the Commonwealth jurisdiction despite the availability of the industrial court and numerous

---

[1] Mr. J. Hills, Secretary of the Coal Industry Tribunal, comments: "... Boards of Reference play an important role in the settlement of day-to-day disputes under a number of federal awards and ... except in cases where a Board exceeds the functions assigned to it, the parties would be most reluctant to upset the system." (Letter to this writer dated December 8, 1964.)

boards of reference. It seems also to be true in Western Australia where both an industrial court and boards of reference are available, and in Queensland where there is an industrial court but no boards of reference. It certainly is true, as would be expected, in New South Wales where there are neither boards of reference nor nonarbitral industrial courts.

DESIRABILITY OF STATE BOARDS OF REFERENCE

It seems surprising that the board of reference still is non-existent, intrastate, in two of the four "arbitral state" jurisdictions, New South Wales and Queensland. In these two states as well as in the other jurisdictions, over the half century since the emergence of the Australian arbitral systems, the number of industrial disputes "arising under" awards has greatly increased as the number of awards has increased. This natural multiplication of disputes over grievances has added greatly to the work load which the tribunals have had to carry. Interest disputes, which also have greatly increased in number, have necessitated great increases in tribunal personnel.

The emergence since 1957 of non-arbitral industrial courts in the Commonwealth, Western Australia, and Queensland jurisdictions appears to have lightened the load upon the award-making tribunals, perhaps most of all in Queensland where there are no boards of reference. But the existence of the nonarbitral courts does not seem to have eliminated the need for boards of reference. Evidently both types of tribunal are needed. Disputes about the meanings of award provisions and matters of enforcement seem appropriate for industrial courts, while disputes regarding tenure (e.g., discharge, layoff, transfer, etc.) may be more satisfactorily dealt with by tripartite boards of reference—and perhaps quite as satisfactorily by one-man reference boards.

In the Commonwealth jurisdiction the Industrial Court, since 1957, has shared with the federal reference boards and even with the Arbitration Commission the responsibility for dealing with some types of rights dispute. The boards, the court and the Commission all settle disputes involving tenure of employment. The court now seems to have exclusive jurisdiction over rights disputes involving the interpretation of award provisions, from dealing with which the boards, as well as the Commission, seem to be practically foreclosed.

In Queensland and Western Australia the recent creation of industrial courts, limited to the exercise of judicial functions, seems to have removed from the award-making tribunals in those states some part, but by no means all, of the responsibility of the "non-judicial" tribunals in relation to disputes on rights.

With all this, there seems to remain a vacuum in the other two arbitral states, New South Wales and Queensland, so far as special provisions for dealing with rights disputes are concerned. In New South Wales the putative handicap resulting from the absence of boards of reference is no doubt greatly lessened by the circumstance that in that state there is not only an industrial commission of ten or twelve judges, but also provision for a wide sharing of responsibility for the determination of industrial disputes through the functioning of two classes of award-making ancillary tribunals: conciliation commissioners and conciliation committees. Both of these classes of "fringe" tribunals evidently may handle industrial disputes on rights; it has been noted that the Commission itself definitely reaches such disputes, both big and little. However, there would seem to be good reason for Queensland, and possibly also New South Wales, to give some consideration to the advisability of setting up boards of reference for disputes "arising under" their intrastate awards.

Award Provisions for Dealing with Intraplant Grievances

There is no question that both Australian unions and Australian employers have largely neglected the problems of worker morale at the local plant level. This is testified to by both Australian and American writers who have been quoted at some length.[2] Both union and company officials generally have been so preoccupied with their logs of claims before the tribunals that the worker at his workplace, and the often acute problems he faces there, are largely forgotten. That this is so seems to be confirmed in at least two ways: most obviously and disruptively by the unusually high proportion of Australian strikes which last for one day or less, and which are mostly precipitated by local grievances at the shop level, and less overtly by the extreme rarity of award provisions for the settlement of grievances. Australian awards incorporating "grievance steps," such as those of the Engineering (Oil Companies) Award, are rarities. There is good reason for thinking that, at a future time when most industrial awards surely will contain either grievance-procedures clauses or board-of-reference clauses, or both, the one-day walk-off will be a minor and not a major type of direct action Down Under. Another potential benefit may well be some lightening of the load of rights-disputes cases on the dockets of the boards of reference, the industrial courts and other industrial tribunals.

---

[2] *Supra,* pp. 108–110 *et seq.*

Appendix A:
The Cases

Case	*Arbitral Tribunal*
The Dobb Case	Supreme Court of New South Wales
The Farthing Case	Commonwealth Boards of Reference
The Boning Room Cases:	
Cairns Meat Export Company	Federal Commissioner
Borthwick Company	Boards of Reference
The Queensland Coal Miner's Case	Commonwealth Coal Reference Board for Queensland
The Cornwall and Sunrise Mines Case	Commonwealth Coal Reference Board for Queensland
The Wool Presser's Case	Industrial Magistrate
The Table Margarine Case	Commonwealth Industrial Court
The "Dumpy Little Hausfrau" Case	Commonwealth Industrial Court
The Overtime-Rate Case	Commonwealth Industrial Court
The Dining Room Case	Commonwealth Conciliation and Arbitration Commission
The Working Alleyway Case	Commonwealth Conciliation and Arbitration Commission
The Builders' Labourers Case	New South Wales Industrial Commission
The Meal Money Case	Commonwealth Conciliation and Arbitration Commission
The Sacking for Smoking Case	Western Australian Court of Arbitration
The Lima Crane Case	Industrial Commission of New South Wales
The Queerah Works (Falls) Case	Commonwealth Conciliation and Arbitration Commission

126

Appendix B:
The Statutes

The Commonwealth
  Conciliation and Arbitration Act, 1904–1964
  Public Service Arbitration Act, 1920–1960
  Stevedoring Industry Act, 1956–1963
  Coal Industry Act, 1946 ("Twin" Statute)

The "Arbitral" States
  New South Wales
    Industrial Arbitration Act, 1940–1961
    Coal Industry Act, 1946 ("Twin" Statute)
  Queensland
    The Industrial Conciliation and Arbitration Act, 1961
  South Australia
    Industrial Code, 1920–1963
    Public Service Arbitration Act, 1961
  Western Australia
    Industrial Arbitration Act, 1912–1963
    Mining Act, 1904–1963

The Wages Board States
  Tasmania
    Public Service Tribunal Act, 1958
    Wages Boards Act, 1920
  Victoria
    Labour and Industry Act, 1958
    Public Service Act, 1958
    Teaching Service Act, 1958

Appendix C:
Selected Bibliography*

Anderson, George. *Fixation of Wages in Australia.* Melbourne: 1929.

Baker, W. A. *The Commonwealth Basic Wage, 1907–1953.* (Issued by the Metal Trades Federation), Sydney: September 1953. Pamphlet.

Barry, Jno. V. "Industrial Regulation in Australia," 1 *University of Queensland Law Journal,* December 1948, 13.

Commonwealth of Australia. *Conciliation and Arbitration Act, 1904–1964.* Canberra: Government Printer.

———. Department of Labour and National Service. *Industrial Relations in Australia, Information Papers,* November 1963. Pamphlet.

———. *Industrial Disputes in Australia.* Canberra: Commonwealth Government Printer, 1958. Pamphlet.

———. *Industrial Information Bulletin.* (Monthly)

———. The Parliament of the Commonwealth of Australia. Department of Labour and National Service. *A note on some aspects of conciliation and arbitration in the Commonwealth.* Canberra: Commonwealth Government Printer, 1958.

Commonwealth Bureau of Census and Statistics. *Labour Reports.* (Yearly)

———. *Industrial Information Service.* (Monthly)

de Vyver, Frank. "Australian Boards of Reference," 10 *Labor Law Journal,* May 1959, 317–329.

Dey, Jno. F. (and others, Editors). *An Outline of Industrial Law* (Commonwealth and New South Wales). Law Book Co. of Australasia, 2nd ed. 1965.

Dunphy, E. A. and Wright, S. C. G. "The jubilee of industrial arbitration in the federal sphere," 25 *Australian Law Journal,* September 20, 1951, 360–378.

Eggleston, R. M. "Industrial Relations," Chapter VIII (pp. 221–246) in *Essays on the Australian Constitution* (Rae Else-Mitchell, ed.) Sydney: Law Book Co. of Australasia, 1961.

Evatt, H. V. "Control of Labour Relations in the Commonwealth of Australia," 6 *University of Chicago Law Review* 1939, 529–551.

Fitzpatrick, Brian. *The British Empire in Australia.* Melbourne: Melbourne University Press, 1941. (Chapter VI: "Labour relations, 1860–1912")

Foenander, Orwell deR. "The achievement and significance of industrial regulation in Australia," 75 *International Labour Review,* February 1957, 104–118.

---

* This list makes no pretension to completeness. It merely sets out some of the items which this writer has found helpful.

——. *Better Employment Relations and Other Essays.* Sydney: Law Book Co. of Australasia, 1954.

——. *Industrial Conciliation and Arbitration in Australia.* Sydney: Law Book Co. of Australasia, 1959.

——. *Industrial Regulation in Australia.* Melbourne: 1947.

——. *Studies in Australian Labour Law and Relations.* Melbourne: Melbourne University Press, 1952.

Gordon, Barry. "Industrial Relations Procedures in an Australian Industrial Complex," note, 5 *Journal of Industrial Relations,* 1963, 160.

Hagger, A. "The Arbitration Court in the 1950's," *Australian Quarterly,* June 1958, 42–56.

Hancock, W. K. *Australia.* Sydney: Australasian Publishing Co., Pty., Ltd., 1931.

Hawke, R. J. (Research Officer, ACTU). "The Commonwealth Arbitration Court—Legal Tribunal or Economic Legislature," 3 *University of Western Australia Annual Law Review* 1954–56, 422–478.

Higgins, Benjamin. "Wage Fixing by Compulsory Arbitration—The Lesson of Australia," 18 *Social Research* 1951, 335–369.

Higgins, Henry Bournes. *A New Province for Law and Order: Being a review ... of the Australian Court of Conciliation and Arbitration.* London: Constable, 1922. (Based on three articles in the *Harvard Law Review:* November 1915, January 1919 and December 1920)

——. *A New Province for Law and Order: Industrial Peace Through Minimum Wage and Arbitration.* 29 *Harvard Law Review,* November 1915, 13–39. (The first of three articles)

——. "Industrial Peace in Australia, Through Minimum Wage and Arbitration." *Monthly Review* of the U. S. Department of Labor, February 1916, pp. 89–110. (Reprint of "A New Province for Law and Order," *Harvard Law Review,* November 1915.)

Isaac, J. E. "Penal provisions under Commonwealth Arbitration," *Journal of Industrial Relations,* October 1963.

Kerr, J. R. "Work Value," *Journal of Industrial Relations,* March 1964.

Kirby, Sir Richard. "Some Comparisons Between Compulsory Arbitration and Collective Bargaining," 7 *The Journal of Industrial Relations,* March 1965, 1–17.

Kuhn, James W. "Grievance Machinery and Strikes in Australia," 8 *Industrial and Labor Relations Review,* January 1955, 169–176.

——. "Strikes and Australia's Industrialization," 28 *Australian Quarterly,* September 1956, 56–68.

Latham, Sir John. *The Industrial Power of the Commonwealth Parliament.* Pamphlet. (Address before Victorian Employers' Federation, Bendigo, October 22, 1952.)

Livengood, Charles H., Jr. "The Lawyer's Role in Grievance and Arbitration," 9 *Labor Law Journal,* July 1958, 495.

McCawley, Thomas William. (President, Queensland Court of Industrial Arbitration.) Industrial Arbitration. Pamphlet.

——. "Industrial Arbitration in Queensland," International Labour Review, March 1922.

McLaurin, W. R. "Compulsory Arbitration in Australia." 28 American Economic Review, March 1938.

Martin, R. M. "Governments, Industrial Tribunals and the Rule of Law," 6 The Journal of Industrial Relations, March 1964, 36–49.

Menzies, Robert G. "Distribution of the Industrial ... Powers," Chapter III, Studies in the Australian Constitution (G. V. Portus, ed.).

Merrifield, Leroy S. "Wage Determination Under Compulsory Arbitration: Margins for Skill in Australia." 24 George Washington Law Review, January 1956, 267.

[New South Wales, "Piddington Report"] Final Report of the Royal Commission of Inquiry on Industrial Arbitration in the State of New South Wales, together with Minutes of Evidence. Sydney: 1914. (New South Wales, Parliamentary Papers, Second Session of 1913.)

Mills, C. P. (ed.). Nolan and Cohen's Industrial Laws Annotated (Book I, the Commonwealth: Book II, New South Wales) 2nd ed.

Oxnam, D. W. "Industrial Arbitration in Australia: Its Effect on Wages and Unions," 9 Industrial and Labor Relations Review, July 1956, 610.

——. "Recent Changes in the Western Australian Arbitration System," The Journal of Industrial Relations, July 1964.

Portus, G. V. Australia: An Economic Interpretation (2nd ed.). Sydney: 1933. (Especially Chapter VII: "The Social Laboratory.")

Portus, John H. Development of Australian Trade Union Law. Melbourne University Press, 1958.

Reeves, William Pember. State Experiments in Australia and New Zealand. London: 1902 (2 Volumes).

Ross, G. W. C. "Constitutional History of Industrial Arbitration in Australia." 30 Minnesota Law Review, December 1945, 1–22.

Sawer, G. "Industrial Law," Chapter 12 (pp. 289–313) in George W. Paton, The Commonwealth of Australia, Volume 2 in the British Commonwealth series. London: 1952.

——. "Judicial Power under the Constitution," Chapter III in Essays on the Australian Constitution (Rae Else-Mitchell, ed.). Sydney: Law Book Co. of Australasia, 2nd ed., 1961.

Sorrell, G. H. "The Dispute at Mt. Isa," 37 Australian Quarterly, June 1965, 22–33.

Sykes, Edward I. The Employer, the Employee and the Law. Sydney: Law Book Co. of Australasia, 1960.

——. "Industrial Conciliation, Arbitration and Regulation," 31 Australian Law Journal, December 16, 1957.

——. "Labour Arbitration in Australia." 13 American Journal of Comparative Law, 1964, 216.

————. "Labor Regulation by Courts: The Australian Experience," 52 *Northwestern University Law Review*, September–October 1957, 462.

————. "The Role of Law in Industrial Relations," 29 *Australian Quarterly*, June 1957, 21–28.

————. *Strike Law in Australia*. Sydney: Law Book Co. of Australasia, 1960.

Thomson, D. C. "Conciliation in the Commonwealth Jurisdiction," 2 *University of Queensland Law Journal*, November 1952, 30.

————. "A Survey of the Australian Industrial Tribunals," *Industrial Law Review*, July 1955.

Timbs, Joseph N. *Toward Wage Justice by Judicial Regulations: An Appreciation of Australia's Experience Under Compulsory Arbitration*. Paris: 1963.

[Victoria] *Interim Report . . . of the Board of Inquiry Appointed to Examine Suggestions for the Amendment of the Factories and Shops Acts*. Melbourne: Government Printer, 1946.

Walker, Kenneth F. *Industrial Relations in Australia*. Cambridge, Mass.: Harvard University Press, 1956.

———— (ed.). *Unions, Management and the Public: Addresses to the First Labour Management Conference at the University of Western Australia, October 8, 1955*. Perth: University of Western Australia Press, 1956.

107